GETTING DIVORCED WITHOUT LOSING YOUR MIND

GETTING DIVORCED WITHOUT LOSING YOUR MIND

How to Manage Your Stress,
Your Ex, Your Budget, and
Get What You Need in Your Divorce

Corey Shapiro

Copyright © 2024 by Corey Shapiro

All rights reserved. No part of this book may be used or reproduced in any manner without written permission from the author.

Editor: Donna Frazier Glynn
Copy Editor: Brijit Reed
Cover Designer: Spoon+Fork, Inc.
Interior Design and Typeset: Susan Shankin
Author Photograph: Sasha Chou Photography

This book contains material protected under international and federal copyright laws and treaties. No part of this publication may be reproduced, distributed, or transmitted in any form or by any means, including photocopying, recording, or other electronic or mechanical methods, without the prior written permission of the author, except in the case of brief quotations embodied in critical reviews and certain other noncommercial uses permitted by copyright law. For permission requests, email the author at: feedback@gettingdivorced.org.

ISBN 979-8-9855921-1-5 (Paperback)
ISBN 979-8-9855921-0-8 (ebook)

First edition.
Printed and bound in the United States of America.

Contents

Introduction		1
Chapter 1	What Is a Difficult Divorce?	7
Chapter 2	Your Emotional Tool Kit	13
Chapter 3	Focus on What You Can Control	31
Chapter 4	Become Less Defensive	47
Chapter 5	Understanding the Divorce Budget	63
Chapter 6	Learn Divorce Attorney Tactics	85
Chapter 7	Accept that the Court Is Always Right	99
Chapter 8	How to Find the Best Attorney for You	109
Chapter 9	Becoming Persuasive	117
Conclusion: Putting It All Together		127
Acknowledgments		133
About the Author		135

Introduction

GETTING MARRIED can be the start of the most wonderful and devastating journey you'll take with someone.

A good marriage can be a secure home base for a couple and a haven for their children, but a bad marriage can dissolve into what feels like limitless pain and despair. It can scar people's lives for years, decades, and even lifetimes.

Until I was 8 years old, I thought I had been born into a family secured by my parents' happy marriage. We were living in Hawaii—and growing up in Hawaii, as Larry David would say, is "pretty... pretty... pretty... good."

However, my world was flipped upside down when I came home one day from third grade and my older sister, Brynne, opened the front door and told me that Mom wasn't home. How could that be? Mom was always home. This was as reliable as the sun rising in the morning.

After that, I experienced the turmoil of divorce from the inside, as a helpless observer. I couldn't save my mom from the anguish, bitter fighting, financial hardship, and sleepless nights that came once she walked out. I couldn't keep her from losing her peace of mind in her divorce—but I can help you. I have devoted the last two decades of my practice to helping people make better decisions in their divorces and minimizing the kind of suffering my family went through.

For some of my clients, making good decisions under pressure comes naturally. Maybe they have a special gene that allows them to make the right moves under extreme stress, but most people aren't hyperfocused mutants. They're normal humans who are just trying to do the best they can under difficult circumstances. Worn down by the tensions of divorce, most people get emotional, say or do things they don't mean, and make impulsive decisions that they will later regret.

However, these responses aren't hardwired—most of them flow from bad habits, and you can regain control by replacing them with new, healthy habits that keep you more centered, more sane, and less reactive.

It makes sense to make these adjustments in your thinking and behavior because the real battle in a divorce is not between you and your spouse but between the negative versions of you both (and the negative versions of your attorneys). When all of you are on your worst behavior, everything feels like a life-or-death situation, where primitive survival-thinking rules.

Resolving a difficult divorce is not wrestling, where you win points for "taking people down to the mat." It's about achieving long-term goals and using the least amount of resources to do it. Think of this book as a kind of a jiu jitsu primer to help you stop wrestling and start winning. It's full of tools and techniques to help you come out ahead in a "battle" where the whole point is to use only as much energy as is necessary to have the other side submit or tap out.

When I check in on clients and ask how they're doing after experiencing a difficult divorce, the best thing I can hear is that "things are quiet." It's then that I know that they're moving back into their better selves and

Introduction

getting on with the business of living the life they were meant to live.

The goal of this book is to help you give your thinking a hard reset in the midst of conflict over issues that can trigger you in every way imaginable.

It is maddeningly difficult to overcome bad thinking and negative reactions when you're triggered, because it feels as if you have no other options available to you, but the payoff is enormous. Instead of burning through money, time, and sanity in scorched-earth maneuvers that don't come close to achieving your most important goals, you can calmly get what you need.

When things broke down between my parents, my mother's emotions told her that her only option was to walk out of her marriage and leave her kids behind. In reality, she had so many other choices in the weeks and months (or even years) leading up to her decision, right up to the moment at the airport when she was waiting for her flight back to the mainland. I wish she had stumbled on a resource like this and had been able to look through clearer, calmer eyes before she made up her mind.

You have many more choices than what your emotions may be telling you—better choices—and I hope you'll use this book to help you see what they are.

I can help you make better decisions under pressure. Learning how to do that doesn't guarantee that you'll have an easy divorce, but it gives you the best chance of having a successful one so you can move ahead, confident that you have what you need to build a new life for yourself and your children.

● ● ●

How it works: your lawyer plays the "outer game" of divorce—you play the inner one.

A CONTESTED DIVORCE, one that's worked out with a judge in the court system, proceeds on two parallel tracks.

One track, driven largely by your attorney, involves every legal action you have to take to get divorced. Succeeding on that track obviously requires technical knowledge of the law in your state or country. It also requires an understanding of court procedure, familiarity with the judge's court rules and preferences, and the ability to read and respond to the attorney your spouse picks to represent them in your divorce.

This book is not focused on that track except to say that as you navigate it, I hope you will retain a divorce attorney who becomes your trusted advisor. (See Chapter 8 for guidance on how to recognize and choose the best lawyer for you.) If you don't trust your divorce attorney, or if you view him or her as nothing more than a person who can render quality legal services on demand, then you may not be using them to your best advantage. A trusted advisor can go beyond performing the technical tasks of the divorce to translate what is happening into practical language, providing you with insight into the immediate and long-term consequences of every action in your divorce.

With a trusted advisor by your side, you will substantially increase the chances that you'll make sound decisions—without losing your mind.

The second track of your divorce—which is the subject of this book—deals with the mental and emotional

Introduction

side of the divorce process—the *inner* level of your divorce journey.

My mission is to give you the profound advantage that comes from being able to think sanely and strategically about your divorce, especially if it involves children. You'll face pressure tactics and strategies designed to push you off balance and keep you mired in unproductive distractions, but as you develop a stronger mindset, you'll be much better at being able to cope, to strategize, and to keep things in perspective. I can't guarantee that you'll get everything you want in your divorce, or that you won't be pushed to your emotional brink at times, but this process *will* ensure that you are doing everything you can to increase the chance of a level-headed divorce—one in which more of your needs are being met.

I have been fortunate enough to guide many clients through contested divorces, and the people who have mastered the approach in this book have not only achieved more in their divorce than they thought possible, but they have also created the most satisfying postdivorce lives for themselves and their children.

Stress, frustration, and strong emotions are to be expected in a contested divorce, but losing your sanity isn't. You can stay positive, powerful, and even peaceful most of the time if you learn to focus your energy exclusively on getting what you need while letting everything else roll off your back. There's no way to do this perfectly, but the six steps I'll show you will help keep you tethered to what matters without losing your composure when things seem to spin out of control.

I hope this book will become a companion throughout your divorce. Use it to remind yourself of who you want to be now, and when this is all over, the *best* version of yourself, building a satisfying new life one step at a time.

Please Note: This book is intended to provide a broad general overview of the mental side of a contested divorce. It is not a substitute for obtaining legal advice and representation for your unique situation from a qualified attorney who is licensed to practice law in your state or country.

Chapter 1.
What Is a Difficult Divorce?

A difficult divorce is an emotional battle. Think of it as the "extreme sports" version of divorce, with patterns and rules that are unlike those in a typical marriage breakup. To survive and thrive in this arena, you can't rely on what you've habitually done, or respond on the fly without thinking. You'll need effective, efficient strategies to neutralize the tactics you'll encounter. Using them takes focus and determination, but once you understand the game being played, you can stay in it while minimizing the drama.

HERE'S WHAT YOU should know about how your high-conflict divorce differs from a typical one.

1. A typical divorce primarily focuses on solutions.

In a typical divorce, couples are focused on creating solutions. Most people want to move on with their lives and conserve their budget (time, emotions, energy, and finances). They may act out at times and experience unproductive thinking, but they are able to move past their emotional roadblocks and enter into a settlement that satisfies them both.

Because of that, in a typical divorce, you can be authentic in asking for what is important to you. Your requests are viewed as reasonable and will likely be considered in good faith. For example, if you were the primary parent during the marriage and took care of the children while your spouse was working 70 hours a week outside the home, you can expect that you will likely have primary custody without too much pushback postdivorce.

2. In a difficult divorce, the primary focus is on unresolved emotional issues.

To put it another way, a difficult divorce uses conflict as a strategy. The other side *creates* problems to ratchet up the pain you feel rather than trying to find solutions. Because of the focus on conflict and the bad behavior of the past, you cannot expect your spouse to accommodate your reasonable requests.

For example, if you were the primary parent during the marriage and your spouse worked 70 hours a week outside the home, you can expect them to request equal or primary custody of the children during a difficult divorce. You can also expect your spouse to engage in other activities that are aimed at making you lose your mind, which can trigger counterproductive behavior.

For instance, early in the divorce process, after retaining counsel, your spouse could seek counseling and tell their therapist they fear that you're abusing the children. Since mental health counselors are required to report any suspicions of abuse, and since they're generally sympathetic people who presume that their clients are telling the truth, they may feel obligated to report such concerns to a child protective agency, which will investigate these claims.

It doesn't necessarily matter that these child abuse allegations will come back as unfounded. The fear, anxiety, and stress of being interviewed by Child Protective Services and/or the police will either force most people to seriously consider rushing to settlement or motivate them to fight to the bitter end.

If you settle quickly, you will most likely have to agree to unfavorable terms, and if you fight to the bitter end, you most likely will not make it through trial because you will have burned through your budget.

The only antidote to this dilemma is to use tactics, tools, and strategies to build your mental strength to keep you from falling into emotional quicksand and help you manage your budget—even when it feels counterintuitive.

3. The experiences of people in a difficult divorce are very different from those in a typical divorce.

In a typical divorce, you may hear the following:

- We resolved our divorce amicably in mediation.
- We put our children first.
- It wasn't that bad; we behaved.
- We were collaborative.

Contrast that with what you hear in a difficult divorce:

- You won't believe the nightmare I'm living.
- I'm so exhausted.
- I fear for my children.
- I'm stuck.
- The kids are being used against me.

4. Solution-focused strategies are not effective in divorces driven by conflict.

One maddening irony you'll have to accept is that your rational strategies for coming up with solutions won't work against a spouse whose mindset is "my way or the highway" or "win at all costs." To get their way, some spouses would rather pay their attorney more in legal fees than what they would have to pay their spouse in a settlement. A conflict-driven spouse who believes that she should retain most of the value of the marital home, even though the law says otherwise, would rather spend $50,000 in legal fees than pay you $30,000. Likewise, if your spouse does not have the financial means to litigate, she'll soon learn that the law will probably obligate you to pay some or most of her legal fees in the divorce. She may then find an attorney who is willing to run up substantial fees by fighting every little issue under the sun. At trial's end, you may get caught in self-interested maneuvering by both attorneys that results in you paying her lawyer's exorbitant fees even though that attorney did little to benefit her—aside from helping her punish you by running up the bill. This is a figure eight that's hard to get out of without a deep understanding of the needs and interests at play. Your best move is to defuse the emotions that are driving this punishing behavior.

5. Despite appearances, the odds are in your favor if your difficult divorce can be settled on mutually agreeable terms.

Spouses in difficult cases fall into two groups. The largest consists of people who have negative personality traits that flare up occasionally due to triggers that unleash their evil twin—their shadow side. While they may at times act disagreeable, manipulative, and even ruthless, depending on their motivations and triggers, they're also

What Is a Difficult Divorce?

able to be kind, considerate, and flexible in your divorce, which moves both parties to a satisfactory settlement.

A much smaller group have full-fledged, diagnosable personality disorders—they're narcissistic, borderline, antisocial, histrionic, or something else. Such disorders may make your spouse so inflexible that they are unable to adapt to the shifting tides in a divorce—the give and take necessary to reach a satisfactory settlement. They may have no light personality traits to counteract the dark ones, so what you're left with is an impasse, where your only hope for an equitable result is to have an arbitrator, like a judge, to help you move on with your lives.

Think about which "devil" you're dancing with in your divorce. If your spouse has occasional negative personality traits, you have a 95% chance that your case will settle without the need for trial. If your spouse has an untreated personality disorder, you have a 5% chance that your case will settle.

Remember these figures and plan accordingly.

> **KEY POINTS:** What Is a Difficult Divorce?
>
> - You know you're in a difficult divorce when the primary focus is the conflict rather than the resolution.
> - Coming out ahead in a difficult divorce requires finding ways to bring out the humanity in the other person so that you won't have to fight with their irrational shadow side.
> - If you're dealing with a spouse who has more than temporary dark personality traits that come out when triggered, such as a diagnosable personality disorder, the odds are against a mutually satisfactory settlement, so save your budget (energy, time, money, emotion) for focusing on the trial.

Chapter 2.
Your Emotional Tool Kit

Most people say they want a fair divorce. The problem is that there is no objective definition of what's fair. You can ask your lawyer what a fair outcome would be, but lawyers are biased. They base fairness on the law, your risk tolerance, and the size of your legal budget (or your lack of one). You can ask friends and family, but they probably base fairness on their own personal knowledge. "Fairness" is thus a hazy concept. So rather than focusing on obtaining a fair result, focus instead on *achieving what is important to you*. To identify your genuine core needs, you'll have to dig deep and look not just at surface issues like money, but at factors like emotions—yours and your spouse's.

Determine what's important.

Determining what's important to you is crucial, so I suggest we take some preliminary actions to help you get a broad overview (and an *inner* view) of what you want, what you need, and what you'll have to do going forward.

First of all, understand yourself.

When prospective clients come in for a consultation, it's not always easy to sort out what they need because so many of them are used to speaking indirectly about their feelings, so they're not always clear about their needs. Everyone has a different way of communicating. Some people don't mean what they say or say what they mean, and most struggle to get past a catalog of fears and resentments.

As I sit and listen to my clients, I work to understand things from their perspectives and then reframe their basic stories in language that gets at the essence of their hopes and fears—without getting caught up in the details. For example, if a client with two homes tells me that they need a divorce because their husband is doing drugs but they're scared of going through with it because of financial issues, I might repeat the heart of the story back to them this way:

"What I am hearing is that you need peace, and one way of getting it is through a divorce. However, if you get divorced, you're worried that you may not have financial peace. You're concerned that you might gain emotional peace but sacrifice financial peace, so you still may not find equilibrium postdivorce." I would, at this point, continue, saying, "I hear you have a second home. As a potentially short-term solution, would you consider moving into the second home to give you emotional distance but also maintain your financial peace?"

When I articulate things this way, helping people step back and see the broad outlines of the emotional landscape without going into the details that trigger them, they sometimes (not always) listen and understand their options better than when they were just focused on a list of grievances, facts, numbers, and logistics. They're more likely to hear and receive my advice, even though they may have ignored similar advice from others.

How do you give yourself this kind of perspective? Pay attention to your emotions.

Your attorney isn't your therapist, but an attorney who is your trusted legal advisor has very practical reasons for helping you work consciously with the emotional level of your divorce from the outset. Emotions complicate everything. When you begin to get in the habit of looking at them directly from the start, you can avoid the costly eruptions and distractions that so easily multiply the amount of time and money you'll have to spend on the process.

In fact, my experience has shown me that the people who have the least costly divorces spend the most time addressing their emotions before thinking about other areas. This is especially true in difficult divorces, where emotions are so often a controlling factor in the outcome.

Here are five starting point questions I use with my clients that can help you gain emotional clarity for the decisions ahead:

1. How much anxiety and stress are you feeling right now?

2. What have you done to decrease your levels of anxiety and stress? Is what you're doing helpful to you not only in the short term, but in the long term as well?

3. If you're only engaging in activities that reduce your stress and anxiety in the short term—such things as shutting down, fighting, or fleeing—do these short-term solutions also help you achieve your long-term goals?

For example, perhaps you've been bickering constantly with your spouse and have decided to simply shut down and not respond to them at all. That helps you get some immediate emotional space, but how will you interact with this person in the future if you have to coparent? When you look ahead, how effective do these short-term strategies seem?

4. What are three things that you want for your life in 3 years?

5. What is one thing you can do today—something you can accomplish without much stress or anxiety—that will move you even just 1% closer to that longer-term divorce goal?

These questions can give you insight into what's driving your behavior, and they're surprisingly useful all the way through the divorce. They'll not only help you stay connected to what's most important to you, they'll help you pay attention to how your ongoing emotional strategies are (or aren't) helping you.

Get Help from Specialized Experts

When people think of getting married, they think of jewelers and florists and wedding venues and Instagram stories. When they think of divorce, they think of lawyers. But to broaden your perspective and your understanding of what you really need and want in your divorce, I suggest that even before you go to a lawyer, or at least before you go to court, you assemble a "divorce team." In addition to your lawyer, you'd be wise to consult with a financial advisor and, if you have children, a child custody expert. Choose people you can trust and respect. If you're anything like me, when someone tells you to do something and you don't want to do it, your first response is *Why?* However, if you believe that this person is knowledgeable and an expert in their chosen field, you might be more inclined to listen to their advice and reap the benefits. Find someone you're willing to *listen* to.

The financial advisor: If you're worried about your budget in your postdivorce life—which most people are—seriously consider consulting a financial advisor at the beginning of the process. Whether you're afraid of ascertaining the numbers that reveal what you have and need or you already have a CPA tracking your every penny, try to get objective information before your emotions take over and make your thinking—shall we say—less than clear. Sit down with your financial advisor, preferably a Certified Financial Planner or Certified Divorce Financial Analyst, and conduct a financial MRI to see what your postdivorce life looks like.

Please do this *before* you consider a life-changing divorce. That meeting should give you more clarity on the resources you will need to move forward with your life and what you genuinely need to bargain for.

The mental health professional: The most hotly contested issues of your divorce may not be confined to money. They may involve parenting issues. To give yourself a greater understanding of those issues, I suggest meeting early in the process with a child custody expert, such as a mental health professional who routinely handles custody issues in divorce courts. You will learn first-hand what the custody determination process is like and how to get the best outcome. This insight will give you a clear picture of what you'll need in order to move beyond gridlock and into solutions that will help you better coparent and care for your child after the divorce.

Know What You're Fighting for and Let That Sustain You as Things Get Tough

A high-conflict divorce can involve years of battle, abuse, and strain. You will have to dig deep, and then even deeper, to get what you really need. That requires strong confidence and the belief that you have the inner resources to keep going. You'll have to be able to reach another gear (or several) when the going gets tough, and you'll have to go well outside your comfort zone to do this at the level necessary to achieve your goals. You will most likely suffer at least temporarily in pursuit of your postdivorce goals, but you *can* reach the other side intact, or even stronger.

When clients come to me, they usually want a peaceful divorce. They hope the process will be easy, but a part of them knows deep down that it won't be. After all, if it were so simple, why would they be paying $500 for a consultation? What I tell them is that the only way to get peace is to prepare for war, and let's be clear: high-conflict divorce is a form of war, despite what you may hear.

Some clients are better than others at learning how to handle conflict in strategic ways that achieve their long-term divorce goals. What sets them apart is that they are so motivated by what they hope to accomplish that they're willing to do whatever it takes to overcome any resistance to the effort and pain that come with getting it. They might be driven by their desire to be the primary parent to raise their child in a healthy and happy home with clear boundaries and defined schedules—rather than seeing their child raised in a more permissive home where inappropriate movies or late-night sporting events are considered acceptable activities for an 8-year-old.

The only question they ask is "What do I need to do to make this happen?" and they're tenacious, even when achieving such a goal might mean committing 3 years of their life to a process where they will not only be vilified, but they'll have to miss work often and incur legal fees that could pay for part, if not all, of their child's college education.

If you're a pacifist, or do not have the grit and the extra emotional gear that will keep you from giving in to the temptation to "end" the pressure when the going gets tough, my heartfelt suggestion for you is this: give a good-faith effort toward mediation or collaboration at the start of the process, and make one of those paths a precondition to a traditional divorce.

If you *are* ultimately forced to go down the traditional path and litigate, I hope you get either a judge who will act as a quasi-mediator/arbitrator to help you settle your case and help you move on with your life or an attorney who focuses on resolving difficult divorces tactfully instead of amplifying the conflict. When being tactful is the tactic, your attorney will show you how to reframe and redirect the energy that is coming your way so you can *use* it instead of flaming out.

Results Are More Important than Revenge or Quick "Relief"

Whatever you decide to do in your divorce, you'll need to adopt new ways of handling conflict, as well as new ways of thinking, behaving, and responding. From the very beginning, I want you to have a core set of tools and attitudes that will be a lifeline every time you face a new challenge, a new irritation, or a new *WTF* moment that throws you into a tailspin. Use the resources in the survival kit below as often as you can. They may sound counterintuitive, and they will not come naturally, but they do *work*.

Your Emotional Survival Kit for a Difficult Divorce

Tool 1: Boundaries

To do your best thinking, you'll need to create a quiet zone around you that's protected from the emotional chaos that inevitably comes whenever you're in contact with your spouse. First, if you're still living under the same roof, create physical (or physical-like) boundaries. Set clear rules for the times and places in which you'll come in contact with your spouse in order to avoid issues that can be more triggering under face-to-face circumstances. When you do engage in person, use a neutral third party such as a parenting coordinator to help you transition into coparenting or parallel parenting.

At the same time, create digital boundaries. Start by noticing how often you look at emails from your spouse. Do you rationalize reading them by thinking there's no harm done as long as you're not responding to them?

Looking at a triggering text or email inevitably taxes you emotionally and energetically and increases the likelihood that you'll obsess about how your spouse is ruining your life. That quickly depletes the energy and focus you need to stick to your divorce strategy, which is why you shouldn't give your spouse unfettered access to your attention. Instead, choose one or two times a day—maximum—to look at what they send you. (You can use your phone's "Do Not Disturb" mode to keep their texts from displaying until a set time that you choose.)

It's ideal to avoid accessing their messages at the very beginning or end of the day—make that sacred time and claim it for yourself.

Tool 2: The 24-Hour Pause

Anytime you do interact with your spouse—whether you're receiving a request, demand, insult, email, voice message or text—*pause* before you respond.

A good rule of thumb is to wait for at least 24 hours *or more* if one of your spouse's notes or phone messages has set you off more than usual. When the thinking side of your brain has been hijacked by emotional overload, the odds are high that your judgment won't be good.

Know that your spouse's team wants to keep you fuzzy and off balance. They want you to be so wrapped up in the impulses of the moment that you cannot think clearly about what you want and need. In your divorce, you have a mission that could include getting meaningful parenting time or equal division of marital assets, and the other side will do everything in their power to make you feel so stressed that you will act out and make bad decisions. You'll be playing right into their hands if you react on the fly and make threats, give up ground because you're "tired of arguing," or take your kids far away without consent.

You will, of course, regret those decisions years later and wonder why you let yourself act in such a self-defeating way, but in the heat of the moment, it can feel like exactly the right thing to do. That's why the more triggered you feel, the more you will need to pause and give yourself space to calm down and connect with the best side of yourself. It won't feel natural to do this, especially if you've been in the habit of firing off instant responses for years or even decades, and it can be particularly difficult to pause in real time when you're with your spouse, but fortunately, when you've put boundaries in place, most of your communication in the divorce and in your postdivorce life will be done electronically, where it's easier to impose some restraint.

Bottom line: *wait* to press send.

I know that imposing a blanket 24-Hour Pause on all your responses to your spouse is a big shift that will ask a lot of you, but it's actually one of the most efficient ways I know to take back your power and shift the dynamic of the divorce. When you're feeling centered (for instance, right now), ask the following questions to help you evaluate how you've been behaving under fire and motivate you to keep the pause in place:

- Am I responding when I'm emotionally triggered? What's the reason?
- Am I giving myself enough time to calm down before I respond? If not, why not?

- Have I engaged in email or text exchanges with my spouse that only continued the conflict? If so, is this a productive use of my time, attention, and energy?
- When I wait 24 hours to respond, how much different do I feel than when I wait 24 *minutes* to respond?
- Do I need to be respected by my spouse? Is this need not being fulfilled by the way my spouse is communicating with me? How else can I fill this need for consideration? Who or what besides my spouse can give me the respect and affirmation I'm looking for?

Tool 3: Mental Distance

When I give clients the 24-Hour Pause rule, they often struggle with it because as they wait, they don't know how to stop obsessing over past events and interpreting them negatively. When you're caught in negative thought loops, it's natural to start getting emotional and become more reactive about future decisions. In other words, you're more likely to allow what just happened to affect what will happen in the future.

To get out of that trap, I suggest using a couple of mental tricks to gain distance *and* perspective. A great way to do this is to put triggering events in a "bubble." Let's say that in the middle of your divorce you are at work on your parenting day, and as usual, you send your nanny, for whom you pay 100% of the cost, to pick up the children and take them to their after-school activity. You receive a call from the nanny that the children aren't at school because your spouse has already picked them up, even though he is supposed to be looking for a job.

You *could* go ballistic and react in the heat of the moment, but I'd recommend that you pause, put the phone away, and take a couple of deep breaths. In the space of those breaths, imagine the whole scene—your spouse and whatever he's up to, the kids, the nanny—taking place within a snow globe, or encased in a soap bubble. Put the scene in front of you and turn off the audio. The children are okay; your spouse is what he is. This can sit, floating outside of you.

Here's what's *not* happening as you let the episode rest.

- You are *not* catastrophizing about the situation, cataloging your grievances about your thoughtless spouse, or firing off a text telling him to "stop interfering with my parenting time." That's the kind of typical chain reaction that's driven purely by impulse as you interpret events in a negative way ("My husband interferes with my parenting time"). It never lets you get beyond anger.
- You are *not* calling your divorce lawyer to unload your frustrations on the clock.

You have taken the situation out of your head and given yourself a chance to look at it more calmly. You've turned away from it instead of reacting to it. At first, this new kind of change in perspective can be challenging to do when you're accustomed to getting an emotional high from firing back. Remember, however, that you're wasting your energy if you let your emotions go up and down. You're using your energy most efficiently when you "flatline."

Tool 4: Mental Time Travel

When you're in pause mode, it's possible to look at the situation from a completely different vantage point: the future or the past. If you take a trip forward or back in time to tap into a better version of yourself anytime you're stressed, you're much more likely to make higher-quality decisions.

Fortunately, while the triggering situation is in the bubble, you have a chance to take your finger off the reactive trigger and summon the best version of yourself to your decision-making by bringing the perspective of your future or past self into the present. When you do that, you can see the consequences of the action you want to take now—whether it's a nasty remark, a livid email, a threatening text, or an expensive call to your attorney.

Why inject time travel? Because your future and past selves already know how a heated impulse will play out. To access their clarity, you can ask yourself some questions that quickly engage your best thinking. I've borrowed them from Suzy Welch, who calls them the 10-10-10 rule.

Questions to Help You Gain a Future Perspective:

- How will this decision impact my divorce in 10 minutes?

- How will this decision impact my divorce in 10 weeks?
- How will this decision impact my divorce in 10 months?
- How will this decision impact my postdivorce life in 10 years?

Questions to Help You Gain the Wisdom of the Past:
- What impact would be playing out in my divorce if I'd taken this action 10 minutes ago?
- What impact would be playing out in my divorce if I'd taken this action 10 weeks ago?
- What impact would be playing out in my divorce if I'd taken this action 10 months ago?
- What would be playing in my postdivorce life if I'd taken this action 10 years ago?

If you don't like what you see as you visualize the consequences, you have a personal "delete" or "undo" button—you don't have to do anything at all.

You pay a high price when you let other people's behavior dictate your impulses, so why not give yourself mental distance from anything that triggers you? Waiting 24 hours gives you time to sleep on the events to ensure you will take more thoughtful actions. Even if you cannot summon the power to wait a full 24 hours or still want to take that impulsive action, you can at least pause in the heat of the moment and ask yourself those questions from the future or the past.

As you practice giving yourself this new kind of space and perspective, you can upgrade your thinking in stressful situations, which will lead you to engage with your best self and to make smarter decisions.

Tool 5: Staying Grounded

As you get clearer about your divorce goals, and more strategic about how to reach them, be aware that one of the strong emotional factors that can undermine you along the way is *fantasy*. Some of my clients feel that their lives will instantly be better once they get divorced. They fantasize that as soon as the divorce papers are signed, they will be new and improved. More time for socializing. More time for activities. More independence. The truth is that although people *can* do better in a postdivorce life, they don't arrive there automatically, nor do they arrive there by wishing. You must first go well beyond your comfort zone to create a life that works for you. Goals must be set for the life you want. Lay the foundation for it with the decisions you make during the divorce.

You'll find out fairly quickly how hard it is to reach your goals in a contested situation. Even when you manage to define and secure your goals, you'll learn that changes in the future can make the things you fought for seem more onerous or insignificant. The reality is that you'll have to keep working for a happily ever after, and you'll need to base your decisions and goals not solely on the conditions you're in today but also on a realistic understanding of how those conditions could change.

For example, some of my clients can work hard to get what they think is a fair deal on the child support they will pay—an amount that will take care of their children generously while not placing their personal finances under undue strain. They may think that if they lose their job, or suffer some unexpected life reversal, it will be "easy" to go back to court to revise the amount downward, but they may be in for a nightmare. Getting a court to lower their child support payments can be a major challenge.

I've seen people agree to a certain child support number thinking they can make it only to realize that they have more expenses than they originally thought, causing them to scramble each month just to cover their own bills. Once again, getting that number changed isn't easy.

On the other side of the table, clients may think that the emotional stress of battling over money and arrangements for the children is so awful that they give in to threats designed to scare them, and then suffer as they try to scrape by on far less than they were entitled to. They fantasize that everything will be better if they can just get some short-term relief, and they don't think about their long-term plan. What usually happens is that, for a time, everything does seem better, but then they hit the limits of those funds and realize they cannot support themselves any longer. They're back in court, working out what they didn't deal with initially—achieving financial stability.

The truth is, trying to dodge the intense emotional challenges that come with high-conflict divorce will only make things worse. However, you can develop the skill and stamina to cut through the fear, anger, bullying, and posturing, as well as the pretending (theirs *and* yours), and stay focused on what you really need. This will keep you centered enough to run the marathon it will take to get it.

In the pages to come, I'll introduce you to a strategy for detoxing your dealings with your spouse and shifting the emotional dynamics that are always at play beneath the surface as your legal case unfolds. At the center of this highly effective approach is one basic idea: *understanding.*

Tool 6: Your Ultimate Power Play—Understanding

One of the most game-changing moves you can make, right from the beginning, is to pivot from combat mode to a search for common ground by understanding your spouse. Getting to an outcome that gives you what you need to move on with your life hinges on whether or not you can stop treating your spouse as the enemy and start dealing with them human to human. That's not easy when someone is coming at you with barrages of name-calling, judgments, and criticisms, but learning to do it exponentially increases your chances of getting what you want—and that makes it worth all the effort it will take.

KEY POINTS: Your Emotional Tool Kit

- To get what you want in your divorce, you'll need clarity.
- Consult with objective third parties, like financial advisors and mental health professionals, in order to size up your own emotional situation and desires.
- You can also obtain more clarity by thinking about issues from two perspectives, the future and the past.
- Create physical and digital boundaries between yourself and your spouse to create calm space around you.
- Wait 24 hours, at minimum, before responding to any communication from your spouse that triggers you or pushes you off balance.
- Stay grounded by keeping your focus on what you need, and be prepared to have to work for it over the long haul. That's how you'll create a life that works for you.
- Your spouse is a human too. The more you can remember that, the better your odds of success in your divorce.

Chapter 3.
Focus on What You Can Control

In a difficult divorce, you are in a long-term battle with a person who's bent on escalating the attacks on you. Accept that over the course of this ugly scenario you may be pushed to your brink. To increase your chances of obtaining your long-term divorce and life goals you need to think tactically. How? By focusing on what is in your control.

IN YOUR DIVORCE, there will be times when you feel stressed and angry as you find yourself in a legal battle with no end in sight. You may wonder, "How did this happen to me?" Please know that wherever you are in the divorce process, unpleasant emotions are a normal part of the experience, and often to be expected.

What's *also* normal is acting out in response to those feelings, and unfortunately, that's a sure way to prolong and deepen the pain of your divorce. You may feel quite certain that there is no way *you* will be the one to act out. You did nothing wrong and do not deserve this heartache—you're the reasonable one, the calm one. "If anyone is going to lose it in their divorce," you may think, "it will be my (fill in the word) spouse."

However, every day I see otherwise normal, healthy people who have made the same assumption quickly learn that it's hard to refrain from reacting, and even harder to do nothing when you feel threatened, pressured, or attacked, which is the common state of affairs in high-conflict divorces.

So, prepare now to strategically manage your responses and plan for what's coming. Knowing what triggers you and how to tip back into balance when your emotions go wild will keep you acting sane, even when you don't feel that way.

How Things Spin Out of Control

If you are a good-natured person and catch yourself behaving as less than the ideal version of yourself, it's likely that you're having a massive fight-or-flight reaction or your defense mechanisms are engaged below your level of awareness.

For example, maybe you want to relocate back to your home country, but your spouse refuses even though the only reason you came to the U.S. was for the marriage. All your family is back home, and if you were there they could help raise the children in a loving environment where the costs of living are significantly lower than where you reside now. Your children would get more attention than your spouse could ever give them—he doesn't even come home from work until after 7 p.m.

With deep frustration, you realize how challenging a relocation case can be, and that's when a thought comes: maybe you should just leave without your children, even though you are their primary caregiver. That would show your spouse why you want your family's help! Thoughts like this (even if they only cross your mind for an instant) are natural and normal, if guilt inducing, but acting on them is crossing a red line.

There's no shame in having darker thoughts—as long as you let them go.

Another scenario: say you are already in a divorce and realize that the other side is applying more pressure on you than you expected, which is taking its toll. You calm yourself by clinging to the thought that when you get to court, the judge will immediately see your side of the case and push your spouse back. The "facts" appear to be on your side. You are the stay-at-home parent of five children, and your spouse has never taken the children alone on a trip during the 16 years of your relationship. However, as soon as you get into court your husband asks to take the children on a trip without you.

This triggers you instantly. You tell the court that you object to the trip because the children's welfare is at stake. You argue that they cannot be away from you, the primary parent, because their father does not have the capacity to appropriately handle the needs of five children—especially since one of them has special needs. When those arguments have no effect and the judge attacks you for interfering with the children's relationship with their father, you feel lost and confused and just want to end this stupid divorce. Justice will never come your way, you tell yourself, so why waste years of your life in court? Better to get out now, even if you are not getting the child support and maintenance you feel you are justifiably entitled to.

You focus on every bad day you've had in court and all the "signs" that the judge is biased against you, and you start to feel dejected and hopeless. Every cell in your body tells you to take a rash action. Wouldn't it feel *so good* to go down and "chaperone" the children on the vacation so they can be taken care of appropriately? Or maybe you should show your spouse the idiocy of his position by just saying "screw it" and leaving your children behind. Let him have them all! That'll show him what it *really* takes to take care of young children on his own.

This level of pressure, anger, disbelief, and frustration—along with the self-destructive, out-of-control solutions your mind produces to deal with them—are what you are up against in a difficult divorce.

Five Tips for Turning Hot Emotions into Cool, Clear Strategy

The only smart way to deal with all the inner turmoil you're facing is to accept the situation you're in and resolve to look at it with less emotion and more stone-cold strategy.

You can do this by focusing on five tips that I stress (over and over) to my clients.

Tip 1: Prepare for a Long War

Instead of thinking that you will win or lose in your divorce or that your divorce will settle, tell yourself that whatever happens, it will be a long, hard-fought war, and the outcome will be a close call. Remind yourself that you most likely will lose individual battles, but you can still win the war itself. Prepare yourself for being treated unfairly by the court and disrespectfully by the other side. That's what happens in this kind of war.

By putting yourself in this frame of mind, you are developing the grit and space you will need to withstand the pressures of your divorce.

Tip 2: Resist Internal and External Pressure to Act on the Spur of the Moment

Understand that your thinking may be faulty when it stems from a trigger. In many cases, it's likely to tell you that your only recourse is to forget your carefully planned goals and either engage in urgent, irrational, destructive combat (fight) or bow out from the pressure without meeting your divorce goals (flight).

For example, let's say you are in court and the other side wants you to sign a parenting agreement that was just proposed that day. On the surface, it seems semireasonable, but you would like time to review and think about the ramifications, as well as add provisions to the agreement that have been on your mind. However, when the court senses you are close to an agreement, they tell you to go into the hallway and come back with the agreement signed. You try to negotiate in good faith, but the other side won't agree to any of your proposed provisions. The court then comes back to you to ask the status of the agreement. When you say nothing has been signed, you are guilted and pressured into going back to the hallway to work it out.

It takes a lot of inner strength to be clear about your boundaries and stand up to the court graciously, but sometimes you are going to have to take heat to do what you feel is right. Remember: you're in control of your answer when someone asks a question. You're in control of when you say "yes" and when you say "no." Ask your attorney for a simple, nondefensive response you can use in these pressure situations, something like "I want to review this new agreement that was given to me today without feeling rushed and will respond within a week."

Tip 3: Be Hopeful, Even When You Don't Feel Confident

Most clients ask me how things are going during their divorce. They believe that a snapshot summary of where they are in the middle of the process will tell them how the divorce will end in the long term. They think that when they know this, they will have more confidence and not be so stressed with the process. I try to teach them that the "scoring system" in a high-conflict divorce is such that until the case is over, anything can happen— even if you feel you are way ahead or way behind!

In the beginning of a high-conflict case, a lot seems to happen. Everyone is hyped up. Accusations are levied. Motions are made. When you appear in court for the first time, you spend hours of time and thousands of dollars on legal fees, and then all that seems to happen after a lot of back-and-forth between the attorneys is an adjournment of the court date. At the end of the day, you ask your attorney, "What happened?" When I get that question, I don't give a play-by-play recap of the events— my clients are generally too overloaded to process the details at that point, and it's likely that reciting them will only trigger their already heightened emotions. Instead, I put on my divorce-coaching hat and tell them the three vital things that are always true at this opening stage:

Focus on What You Can Control

- Over 95% of what happened today was noise.
- We are not deterred by the roadblocks the other side is erecting in our path to hinder your divorce goals.
- It will be challenging to do so, but we can overcome these obstacles and achieve our goals if we focus on what is in our control.

If this does not help settle their emotions, which are generally high, I stress to them that a big part of their divorce case will revolve around how the other side "creates a frame," which is a technique that all competent divorce attorneys use to try to influence the court. This is more helpful than discussing the details of what happened at this point.

Think of the perspectives being presented as window frames. Each side is trying to get the court to look at the facts of the divorce through its own window frame to emphasize a particular viewpoint and set of information. For instance, as you try to get sole custody of your child, your frame (or the narrative you ask the court to accept) might be that you are the calm, stabilizing force in the child's life and your spouse is an irresponsible vagabond who has never been consistently available to the family. This frame, as I tell my clients, is not necessarily the whole truth, but it is our perception of the truth, the view we want the court to see.

Consistency is key, and if you overanalyze, overthink, and overcomplicate every insult and provocation that the other side is lobbing your way, it will just cloud your thinking. That will distract you from the goal of getting the court to look clearly through your frame. You might, for example, begin acting erratically because you've been triggered and could seriously undermine your otherwise persuasive custody narrative.

I also tell my clients that time changes things, so we should not really give much significance to what happens on a daily (or even hourly) basis. At first, I may think I did well at a hearing, in a court conference, or at oral argument on a motion, but when the judge finally gets around to actually writing a decision, time may have changed his or her perspective. It has happened to me numerous times that judges have told me initially, and in strong terms, that they did not believe in my theory of the case. That has sometimes made me second-guess my theory, but I still advocated and attempted to persuade them to come around to my position once the court reviewed all the evidence in detail. In those situations, it was not uncommon for the court to change its mind and decide to look through my frame.

It's normal to be emotionally upset about what's to come as your case lurches forward in court, no matter how prepared you think you are. If you feel overwhelmed with anxiety about what will come next and none of the above strategies work to bring you back to equilibrium, getting a second opinion may help you see things differently. There is only so much you can learn from your attorney. Maybe a fresh perspective can change your outlook or offer you options that your current attorney does not see. At the very least, obtaining a second opinion can give you the confidence you need to know that you're on the right course, even if things feel shaky. One thing I do not recommend, though, is getting this second opinion from a friend or from an attorney who is not a matrimonial attorney.

Tip 4: Resolve Not to Escalate

No matter what negative or vile thing your spouse says to you, resolve to cloak your response in emotional intelligence. Pick a simple, neutral script and stick to it. It's the most direct way to give yourself an edge.

Start with a few canned phrases to get things going. Think like a politician, and no matter what question is asked, know what answers you want to give. For example, if your spouse says, "You picked up the children late—don't let this happen again or else you won't have parenting time," it will make you want to argue. Instead, you must try restating their position in a neutral way: "You want the parenting plan to be strictly followed." If they're belligerent, you might just think those words to yourself to create some inner space. Keep your responses quiet, calm, and short—or better yet, as the next tip suggests, say nothing at all.

Tip 5: Do Nothing

Very little is in your control in a high-conflict divorce. Once you go to court, it seems it is the judge who has the power. I always tell clients that the further you go into the divorce process, the less control you have because the court makes the ultimate decision on your case. And when you have so little control over your future, it's natural to feel anxious, which is why most cases settle. The trick to overcoming this feeling of powerlessness is to double down on what you *can* control so that you can regroup. One choice that's always under your control, though it's hard for many of my clients to do, is to just do nothing at all.

Doing nothing is difficult because the negative energy being directed your way leaves you pumped up, in the fighting mode. It's hard not to feel fear and fury and want to launch into action when you've been unfairly accused (for example, the other side says you've abused your child). It's natural to want to lash out when the other side or court is disrespectful and mean, or when the other side's attempt at a theory of the case is not based on facts or reason. Unfortunately, what feels like a natural, appropriate reaction when you're upset is likely to be counterproductive and damaging to your case.

Let's say you agreed to a parenting plan, but your ex does not comply with it and you've never had the funds to hire an attorney to enforce your rights, so over the years you've done nothing more than send the occasional email asking your ex to honor the agreement. Finally, you've gotten some funds together and hired an attorney to help you take on the issue, but because money is still tight, you don't hire a process server to serve the court papers you spent thousands of dollars having your attorney prepare. Instead, you give them to the nanny to deliver to your ex. You do not tell her what the papers are about since you don't want to put her in the middle. So the nanny, not knowing the importance of what she is delivering, just gives the papers to your child and tells him to give them to his mother during his next visit with her.

Focus on What You Can Control

When the time comes for the other side to respond to the papers, rather than admit any wrongdoing about not following the parenting plan, the opposition ignores the facts you raised and focuses exclusively on how unethical you are for allowing your child to serve the court papers. They then make a cross motion asking for a change of custody because of your poor parenting choices, even though your ex has never before shown any interest in having overnight parenting time.

This type of heat from the other side is hard to absorb. Doing nothing in response to tactics like this will require you to summon the same kind of restraint that a recovering alcoholic needs to keep from drinking. It takes willpower, but you can build the mental muscles that will help you hold back. Here are some techniques that my clients use to stay emotionally sober and strong enough to *do nothing* again and again.

- Decide that whatever happens, you will do nothing about your divorce when you are triggered. Then, think of a ritual that you will use to calm yourself instead of reacting to a trigger. This ritual could be anything—visualizing yourself on a tropical beach if you only have a few moments, drinking a glass of water, walking around the block, meditating for 10 minutes, starting a 24-Hour Pause by setting a timer on your phone, or a combination of a few of these strategies. The point is, when you use this replacement behavior, you are directly taking control of what happens when you get triggered. You're training yourself to act your best when you're feeling your worst.

- Decide that you will strategize your way through this chess match instead of throwing your pieces at the other side and thinking you can win. Step back so you can evaluate the situation without basing your perspective on your feelings and needs. This provides you with the space you need in order to reframe it in the most useful and positive way possible.

For example, let's say that in the middle of nasty divorce proceedings, you want to go see your father on his deathbed back home in France. Your spouse knows your father well. You were even married in France at your father's home, and your family has traveled there together many times, but now your spouse won't let your child go with you to see his dying grandfather. You end up making a motion in court and spending thousands of attorney dollars to get what you want. It seems to be a simple, reasonable request. At the deadline for responding to the motion, your spouse changes their mind and agrees to let you travel, but the lawyer adds that they just need "some time" to prepare a stipulation to that effect and asks for a short adjournment along with a new date to come back to court.

You ask that the stipulation be prepared while you are in the courtroom right now, as time is of the essence, but the other attorney protests, saying that they want to prepare the stipulation properly. That same day, you have your attorney prepare a two-page draft of the stipulation and send it off to the other side for review. The opposing attorney waits 2 weeks, then comes back with an eight-page stipulation filled with needless boilerplate language and asks that you pay a bond of $50,000 to go to France so you won't be tempted to abscond with the child.

Now, most people will lose it at this point, if they haven't already done so well before, but *you* don't have to. This is where you need to dig deeper. Do it by asking: What's really happening here? Do you think that there's even a whit of concern on the other side that you will run off with the child? Of course not! The legal foot-dragging and the request for a bond have just one purpose: to increase the difficulty of the divorce. The message the other side is sending you says: ***We are difficult—even on small matters. This is going to be a messy divorce no matter what you do, so give in to our demands or we will make your life hell.***

You have choices here. The easiest is to go ballistic, fight back, and fall into their trap. It's also pretty easy to just give in. However, if you can see their strategy for what it is and step back, you can find a way out of this problem that serves and advances your strategy as if you're playing a game of chess—rather than checkers.

Being strategic instead of reactive—and doing it repeatedly—is how you will meet your long- term divorce goals. It's how you will win the war instead of fighting battles so costly that you'll second-guess whether you won at all! What I would tell the client above is "Just go to France without the child during a vacation, when you don't have a parenting responsibility. I know you want the child to see your father, but that's not going to happen now, and the cost for taking that position will be paid someday soon. It's not worth it."

I use the same "wait and reframe" strategy myself. If I am unable to see my client's options in a logical way that turns what seems like chaos into order, I like to take my own 24-Hour Pause or two so my subconscious can process the situation before I respond and act.

During this pause time, I will engage in activities that replenish me so I can come back with a fresh perspective and renewed energy to fight the battles that lead my clients to their divorce goals.

It works for me and it works for my clients as well. It will work for you too.

> **KEY POINTS:** Focus on What You Can Control
>
> - Most people come to divorce in an emotional state. When they see that a litigated divorce is all about losing control of decisions that impact their lives, many spouses settle, and in a vast majority of cases, settling makes sense.
>
> - If you find that your spouse won't come to terms on one (or more) of your reasonable core needs, it may feel as though you have no choice but to press on with your divorce. In this situation, it is helpful to focus on what you can control to help remain in equilibrium so you can make better decisions in your divorce.
>
> - For best results, expect war instead of peace, and realize that the only way to get peace is to prepare for a long war.
>
> - Be hopeful even when you feel there is no chance that you will succeed. Your belief that things are dire may not necessarily be true. Sometimes you just have to keep pushing (and pushing) to get what you think is fair.
>
> - Quite often, you will get the results you most want by doing nothing at all as your attorney pursues your strategy.

Chapter 4.
Become Less Defensive

Your ongoing challenge as the divorce goes on will be to develop many and varied ways of stopping yourself from making bad decisions in the heat of the moment, decisions based on emotions, not logic. Remember: emotional decisions can easily derail your divorce strategies. One helpful solution is to connect with your emotional side to address out-of-control feelings *before* you react. That can be challenging, so I've outlined some strategies you can use to park (or process) your emotional reactions before engaging and reacting. Then, when you do respond, you can do it in a productive way, thus increasing the chances of more favorable results even when the level of conflict is high.

WHEN YOUR SPOUSE does something that upsets you, it's easy to focus on the impact of his or her behavior and make negative assumptions about their intentions. For example, when they drop the children off 20 minutes past the agreed-upon exchange time, you might assume that they are intentionally "gatekeeping," rather than being caught up in unexpected traffic. When the monthly maintenance payment is late, you might assume he or she is trying to ruin your finances, rather than hustling to make the child payments by "robbing Peter to pay Paul."

Those negative assumptions about your spouse's (or ex-spouse's) intentions can be highly destructive and counterproductive. I understood this (in theory), but I did not fully realize how easy it is to fall into this trap until I experienced it myself in a pressurized situation.

One day after a court conference that went my client's way, the opposing attorney asked me to have an impromptu settlement meeting with her and her client in one of the court's conference rooms. When we started the meeting, I assumed we were going to discuss a logical resolution of the matter since we seemed close to a settlement—at least in theory. The opposing spouse, on the other hand, was not ready to think logically. He needed to express himself emotionally. So out of nowhere, he started verbally attacking me, threatening to report me to the disciplinary committee for negotiating unethically.

Although I knew I was being ethical and did nothing wrong, I was immediately put on the defensive—and did not handle it well. Instead of parking my emotional reactions and focusing on why I was being attacked, I went on the attack myself. Like so many of my clients, I just could not see past my own emotional triggers and the story I created about why the other person was attacking me. I jumped to a story that judged this man and was unproductive, at best, in helping my client find a tactful solution to her divorce.

It didn't have to be that way—I had options that could have given me perspective and clarity. When the man began attacking me, I could have taken a break to process my feelings, so I could regain my composure. While processing, I could have thought through why he was acting so angrily—but from *his* perspective, not mine!

Had I done this, I could've seen that he was frustrated about being in court and felt powerless to change the support amount we'd asked for based on his high income. That sense of powerlessness was extremely un-

Become Less Defensive

comfortable for him because he had a need for control and respect, which he was ultimately losing. He did not want to accept the reality of the situation and pay what he considered an unnecessarily high child support and maintenance amount—even though his current attorney (and the previous one) had already agreed with me that it was fair in principle.

His new attorney had asked for the meeting solely to allow him to let off steam (at my expense!). If I had realized that, and if I'd been able to keep from being engulfed by my reactions, I would have been much better equipped to sidestep the attack and neutralize the tense situation. Instead, I sought to defend myself, which forced the man to double down on his own attacks. I was not in a position to be persuasive because I was triggered too.

That made the settlement meeting unproductive and increased the chances of engaging in only black-and-white thinking that left no room for meeting in the middle. Because of this, the only way out was a trial in which we would all lose our minds. Fortunately, the case did settle for the numbers we discussed at that meeting, but not for another few months, which only increased the budget. I learned the hard way how much reactiveness costs everyone and how easy it is to get derailed from our divorce goals.

The lesson for you: When emotions run hot, step away. Process in private and keep returning your focus to what's really behind any negative behavior coming your way. If you've been triggered, don't engage at all, except to say you need a break. Let the emotional wave dissipate and lose its power before doing or saying anything.

The Top Two Ways to *Lose* in High-Emotion Situations

If you ignore or misunderstand the emotional layer of your divorce, you'll probably wind up clinging to two strategies that are guaranteed to fail:

1. Using Facts

In the midst of conflict, reaching for logic is such a natural default that we tend not to question it. It *seems* to make sense to use facts to try to persuade your spouse to be reasonable and do the right thing in the divorce but it doesn't work. Facts speak to the logical part of your brain, and the logical side of the brain is not what needs to be persuaded in a high-conflict divorce. What needs to be persuaded is the emotional part of the brain, which drives behavior. You'll hear me repeat this throughout this book: facts will not change your spouse's mind. If you can engrave that one fact in your mind, you'll be way ahead of the game, and much less frustrated.

2. Using Scare Tactics

When facts fail, we often try to induce anxiety in the other party with insults, threats, and yelling. That is almost certain to trigger your spouse and make you both dig in. If you don't manage your emotions when you're really scared or angry, you only leave yourself three options: to fight (which may mean digging in for long, expensive litigation), to flee (which usually means settling on a fire sale—the skimpiest possible arrangements for support and custody), or to freeze (which usually means not properly preparing for court or trial and letting the chips fall as they may).

Any of those choices will likely have negative long-term consequences in your divorce and postdivorce life.

So, if facts and scare tactics don't work when emotions run high, what does? *Offering the other person understanding* is what works.

A Five-Prong Process to Become Less Defensive and More Understanding

The actions below are not "bold and dramatic," and they may strike you as irritating, useless, or even ridiculous when you're facing hardball tactics and your levels of stress are off the charts. Learning to use them is like practicing a martial art. They'll let you redirect the energy of an opponent who seems far more powerful, giving you the advantage that comes from being able to flip the emotional dynamics in your favor.

Prong 1. Offer Emotional Support

The battles you're having may look like they're about a variety of things, but most of them come down to both sides wanting to feel respected and understood. If you get this and try to look at things from your spouse's point of view, you'll be able to begin humanizing your responses and will have a much better chance of persuading them to move in your direction.

That's why the first step to cooling down a heated situation is to give the other person emotional recognition. When I tell my clients to do this, they think I'm crazy. "Why would I give my spouse anything?!" they ask me. "He's driving *me* crazy. I have to spend so much money and waste so much time because of him—why would I care about his emotional well-being? He should be giving *me* emotional support, but of course, he's incapable of doing that because he's so selfish."

I nod my head and listen patiently because I have heard this response from clients many times over. However, as I work with them, they realize that the best way to decrease the time, energy, money, and emotion they have to invest in the process is to try and give the other side what they need. Offering emotional support is the best way to ensure that they can give *you* what you need in return.

To be clear, when I say "give your spouse what he or she needs," I do *not* mean giving your spouse their stated positions or wishes. I want you to give them what is genuinely important to them on an emotional level. For example, if your opposing spouse wishes to pay $1,000 a month in child support and your lawyer advises you that the law would support paying $3,000 in child support, I am not suggesting that you agree to the $1,000 proposal.

Instead, I want you to help your spouse move away from their position earlier in the process by showing respect and understanding that they'll perceive as sympathetic to their *point of view.* For example, you might sense that maybe your spouse wants to pay only $1,000 in child support because she feels financially strained or angry about having no control over how the money is spent. If you understand where your spouse is coming from, you have a better idea of how to influence them.

How would you express this understanding? I'd suggest starting in places where there's already goodwill. For example, if your ex is paying your child support at a high level, you can show her what you're doing with the money by sharing photos and stories to make her feel included and respected. Don't expect any response. Just know that you are building goodwill. In the tense moments before or after court, you can also say something simple like "This is a challenging time for us, and feeling financially strained isn't good for our family." That may be all you *can* say in that moment, but it's about deescalating emotions and changing perceptions. Depending on the level of conflict and ill will, making progress can take time. Know that you're moving in the right direction, a step at a time.

When my clients understand the concept of offering emotional support, they get better at parking their own emotional responses and processing them later. This makes it easier for them to begin looking at the other person's stated positions to help them understand what's really important to their spouse. As they do that, they have a much easier time staying composed during the divorce, which gives them a better shot at an acceptable resolution. They're far less likely to sabotage themselves through triggered behaviors that cause the court to view them negatively or inflate the costs of their divorce.

Prong 2. Get Them to Say Yes Even on Uncontested Issues

A number of my clients have never been in litigation or high-stakes negotiations. If they had, they would better appreciate how slow litigation can be and how little time the court has to devote to their case. They'd also understand that negotiation is a dance and that certain steps lead to harmony and other steps lead to roadblocks.

The best approach in this process is to start where you can find agreement. Don't just dive in and use all of your energy working to resolve the tough contested issues between you and your spouse (or ex in a postdivorce litigation). This is a futile waste of your resources. Instead of butting heads over major items, such as what amount of maintenance is appropriate, it's best to think of working incrementally to persuade them to give you what you need. This is done by focusing your energy on uncontested issues and getting your spouse to make agreements (or microagreements) on them—things like you keeping the Florida timeshare. Why do you need to have an agreement for issues that are uncontested? Because the more you can agree on issues together, the better the foundation you have for working on resolving the more contested issues together.

As you do this, you're gradually changing the dynamic between you both and tipping it toward cooperation rather than stress and acrimony. This also narrows the issues that the court (or other decision-makers) will have to resolve, saving your budget. When you seem to be at an impasse, whether in negotiation or in everyday life with your spouse, think of flipping the script to give the other side what they want (which is *not* their stated position) so they will give you what you want (which is also not your stated position). Start asking: **How can I offer understanding and respect?** Both of these things are effective, in your control, and free.

For example, although your first thought might be how unreasonable your spouse is being in a negotiation where they request the moon, the sun, and the stars, when you give it a little more time and think about things from their perspective, you may start to see that the issue is really about financial stability, which is also the issue you care about most. The only difference is that you're each approaching it from the opposite position in that you want to pay less and your spouse wants you to pay more.

Prong 3. Listen through the "Noise" for the Values You Share

So, how do you get from impasse to "understanding and respect"? Anytime the other side digs in or goes on the attack, consciously put aside your need to be respected, or to be treated fairly and with dignity. Drop any need to defend yourself by "clearing the air." Instead, ignore anything the other side is expressing that isn't useful (insults, threats, abusive language, etc.). It's all just noise and distraction.

Get out of your emotions and into your rational brain by turning your attention from the differences you have with your spouse to the values you share. This is where you'll find a path to the understanding you need.

Say that early during in the COVID pandemic your spouse wants to take your son outside more to play, but you don't want your little boy out of the house at all unless he's wearing a mask, and neither of you has access to one. Your spouse says you're overprotective and robbing the child of opportunities to play and exercise, saying that he's bored and suffering from being indoors all of the time.

Though it's difficult, look past your spouse's attempts to make you feel like a bad parent (the noise) and shift your focus from the surface-level position they're taking (let the child play outside without a mask), to the values that lie beneath it. At the core, they want your son to be healthy, safe, and happy—and so do you. They believe it's safe enough to go outside without a mask on, and you disagree. In other words, you agree on the fundamental goal (healthy, safe, and happy), but you each have a different position as to what that looks like.

Please note that just because you understand more clearly the underlying reasons for your spouse to take their position, it does* not *mean you agree with their position. It means you acknowledge your common ground.

Simply doing that allows you to think more empathetically about your spouse and puts you in the right state of mind to respond to them strategically. Empathy is the key, so if you're struggling to find the values you share, consider these questions:

- Have I thought about what is important to my spouse? Why are they taking this position? If I look at this position most positively through the lens of common universal values, what values is my spouse expressing in taking this position? Can I admit that I agree with the goal, if not the way to reach it?

- Does seeing that we agree on the common values but disagree on the strategies we both are using to achieve them make me more curious or less curious about my spouse's intentions?

- Am I focusing on what we do not agree on? How does that make me feel? Does it give me a sense of accomplishment?

- Am I ignoring our common ground just because my spouse is acting like a jerk? Is that why I find it so hard to think empathetically about our shared common values? Can I offer understanding, even if it isn't returned, so I can achieve my long-term divorce goals?

Prong 4. Respond in a Strategically Neutral Way

Once you begin to see the shared values beneath your competing positions, you're ready to respond strategically so you can calm and neutralize the situation instead of pouring gasoline on the flames. This does not mean that your spouse will not continue to bait you back into your default self-protective mode. Your spouse probably has deep-seated fears and may view *anything* you do as negative, so do not expect a resolution of your issues, but do expect a deescalation of the conflict you two are living under.

The secret sauce for deescalating is that once you see the values you share, you need to respond more from a place of curiosity rather than a place of judgment and criticism. This is not about being right or wrong. This is about reasonable people disagreeing. If you can make that shift, you can lead your spouse out of their rigid thinking.

To do this effectively, it is helpful to tread lightly with your spouse and to limit what you say to objectively true statements they cannot disagree with.

- The first step is to open your statement in a very neutral way with a soft opener such as "it seems" or "I heard."
- The second step is to list facts they cannot disagree with. In our "play outside" example, you

might open by saying something like "It seems like a scary time now with this virus." You want a quiet opening—nothing tricky or provocative about it.

Prong 5. Ask Questions Instead of Making Demands

The last piece of the puzzle is giving the other side the power and control to resolve "your" problem in the best way possible. Once you give them the understanding and respect they want, they'll be more ready, hopefully, to give you what is important to you. Even if what they offer falls short, at least they will be rethinking their tactics and be more receptive to settlement.

It's important not to demand what you need in a direct way. Instead, enlist them in trying to find a solution to your problem by asking open-ended, clarifying questions that you frame in a neutral, nonjudgmental way so there will be no defensiveness on their part.

Step softly toward them using "it seems," then follow it with true statements they can agree with that can get to the underlying issue. Finally, ask your open-ended question. For the example above, that might sound like this:

"It seems we disagree about how best to care for our child during this pandemic" (underlying issue).

"Covid vaccines are not a guarantee (currently a true statement), and we don't know how any of us will react to the vaccine if we get it" (also currently a true statement).

"How can we make sure our child is safe during these times if we let him out to play, considering the risks involved?" (an open-ended question).

Your question engages curiosity and begins to activate the other person's problem-solving mind.

Become Less Defensive

Notice how different this is from what you might say if you let your less-evolved side lash out: "You know people are dying out there! How can you let our child go out without a mask? Are you trying to kill us all? I forbid it. This is why I will never trust you with custody!" That is escalation at work, and I guarantee you, if you use that kind of language rather than learning a gentler way of speaking, you will have a long, brutal, and costly divorce, so take a deep breath and reread the step-by-step example above. That's the feeling you're looking for.

In a child support situation where your spouse does not want to pay the amount of money required by the law, there might be a tendency to hammer away with statements like "Don't try to get out of it. The law says that's what you have to pay, and you're going to jail if you don't."

Yes, those are the facts, but remember—facts aren't persuasive. You'll only escalate matters and make your opposing spouse feel triggered, which increases their resistance, and in turn, this will increase the spending of your time, money, energy, and emotion on the divorce.

Again, it's far more effective to ease in gently, restating the underlying issues, making true statements, and closing with an open-ended question:

"This is such a stressful time" (true statement).

"It seems we're both concerned about how child support payments will affect us" (underlying issue).

"How can you pay child support in an amount that complies with the law while also maintaining your lifestyle?" (open-ended question).

Such questions are empowering and respectful, and they sidestep a war. Even if there's no answer, or the response you get falls short of your expectations, you are moving from reactive mode to problem-solving thinking, which only increases the chances of a settlement in the near future.

When All Else Fails, Take an Emotional Time-Out

It is hard to change communication patterns, especially if they were ingrained in us as children, so at times you may need to step away to regroup. If you are feeling out of control and want to explode, simply be direct about it so you will not escalate or add to the conflict. You could say: "I need a time-out. I am feeling defensive, and I know that until I calm down, I may only make things worse—which I will not do." Then, take a break and think over how you can use the emotional judo moves above to be less defensive and more persuasive.

KEY POINTS: Become Less Defensive

- Getting defensive only encourages the same reaction in your spouse, making it that much harder to solve problems because everyone is busy defending themselves from perceived attacks versus trying to find a way out of the problem.

- You can redirect the energy that comes your way so that it deescalates your spouse. Do this by giving your spouse what he or she wants, which is emotional support in the form of understanding, respect, and empathy.

- Everyone just wants to be heard, including your spouse. When you're stressed, it's easy to believe that the other person doesn't deserve to have his feelings and humanity acknowledged. Remember that you're not just doing this for them. The emotional support you give your spouse is for *both* of you so you each can find a better way out of the conflict.

- Once you've offered support, try to get your spouse to agree on resolving outstanding issues, even if they are uncontested and small.

- Listen for your mutual values in order to build empathy, then ask open-ended clarifying questions to keep both of you in a problem-solving mode where you'll both be using your best thinking.

- If you find you cannot do this, especially at the beginning of changing decades-long patterns, ask for an emotional time-out and regroup.

See Chapter 9 for a case study showing how one of my clients put these skills together to become more persuasive.

Chapter 5.
Understanding the Divorce Budget

A high-conflict divorce unfolds over time. You're in a marathon, not a sprint. That means you'll have to plan wisely for the long haul and carefully manage all your resources—emotions, money, energy, and time—in order to achieve your divorce goals. The best way to do that is to think about those resources as budget items you need to manage. In your divorce budget, your energy, time, and emotions are as important as your money—and you're the one who will have to plan, juggle, set priorities, and know your limits in every category.

You're the only one who can do this.

YOU'RE PROBABLY THINKING, "Why do *I* have to manage all this? Shouldn't my attorney be helping me steer my divorce in the most effective way possible?" The problem with leaving your divorce budget in your attorney's hands is that he or she can't generalize about the proper resources to invest. Your relationship with your budget is unique to you. Only *you* can decide (ideally before you begin this process) how much time, energy, money, and emotion you can devote to your divorce.

The War on Your Budget: Shock and Awe vs. Attrition

A major factor that will shape your budget is that the other side may try to intimidate you by doing everything it can to deplete your resources. Many clients come to me facing one of two expensive strategies. The first is "shock and awe," a move that some high-powered divorce attorneys like to use to break down your will. They start the divorce aggressively, bombarding you with motions, extreme positions, and demands that must be worked out in repeated trips to the courthouse. You may give in if you can't stomach conflict, especially if your attorney isn't effective at coaching you through that feeling of overwhelm that the opposing side's shock-and-awe strategy can produce. You may also allow yourself to be dragged into a long, extremely costly "arms race" in which you try to retaliate in kind. That's how shock and awe gets the results it wants.

The second strategy, waging a war of attrition, tries to deplete you in a different way. Here, the tactics involve making life difficult for you and wearing you down. Long-standing arrangements involving such things as traveling abroad with a child to visit grandparents are suddenly challenged, creating a flurry of issues that have to be addressed on top of the divorce itself. So much time and money may go into revisiting these issues and distractions that lawyers' fees climb while the divorce process continues to drag. I have seen lawyers bill for *$1 million dollars* in attorney fees before trial, without even conducting a single deposition! That's the equivalent of getting everyone prepped and ready for a heart transplant surgery—the hospital, the doctors, even the patient—and sending the bill, only to announce that there's no heart available.

Why You Need to Prepare for the Worst

The reason for all this concern over budgeting is that divorce litigation puts the parties under such extreme emotional pressure that it's common for people to act out instead of acting rationally. In that sense, divorce cases are like criminal cases. However, in criminal law, the court is dealing with generally bad people at their best. The truism about divorce law is that it's all about generally good people behaving at their worst, and everyone—maybe even you at this point—expects that they'll be the exception. Unfortunately, I've seen genius-level clients who are experts in their fields fall apart in their divorces. Either they want to control every little detail (even though they have no experience in divorce litigation), or they compulsively focus on issues that are not urgent or important.

Let's say Bob's relationship is breaking down and his spouse accuses him of domestic violence. Bob is arrested and a temporary order of protection is granted. When Bob hires a divorce lawyer and they ask the divorce court to give Bob parenting time, his wife opposes the motion, alleging he is an alcoholic and drug addict. The court orders drug testing, he tests positive, and the court allows parenting time supervised by a mental health professional. Three months later, the parties come back to court and Bob is tested again. This time the results come back negative. He then has his attorney request unsupervised parenting time. When the attorney's arguments have no effect, Bob tells his lawyer that he wants to speak for himself and wishes to directly address the judge in open court.

If you were watching this scene and knew what was going on, you would feel slight shifts in the courtroom and notice that for a moment or two, everyone from his lawyer to the judge's clerk works together to keep Bob from talking. Meanwhile, Bob is undeterred. He does not understand that the court system doesn't work the way the rest of his life does, and that even though he is used to special treatment and getting his way, his personal plea for leniency will not work here. In fact, it will only backfire, resulting in a loss of respect the court had for him because he ignored protocol and his attorney's advice. Bob has lost sight of his divorce goals and budget.

Another example is Laura, who wants a divorce but is engaged in a multiyear custody battle with her husband over their 3-year-old child. The parties have two bedrooms and have been using them to sleep separately. However, the second room was originally set up as an office instead of a bedroom, so Laura's husband keeps all his clothes in the master bedroom, where Laura sleeps. He then has to come into that space regularly to get his clothes and other belongings.

When she asks him to remove his belongings, he takes a few of his clothes but leaves the rest behind. Laura becomes furious and tells her attorney to demand that Drake be ordered to remove his things from her space. When the opposing side doesn't respond, Laura is incensed and keeps insisting that her lawyer push the point. She has become obsessed with an item that is of no help in moving her toward her divorce goals. All this battle does is increase her divorce budget.

You can bring more rationality into the divorce process and avoid the inefficient use of your budget if you are religious about spending your resources *only* on actions that move you closer to what you need in your divorce.

Your Divorce Budget, Category by Category

There are countless ways to inadvertently blow more than you ever intended as you work to end your marriage, so let's look closely at each element of the divorce budget to help to ensure that you understand how you can rein in—or inadvertently amp up—the costs.

Managing Your Emotional Budget

To start, put expectations aside and focus on what you can control. When a spouse comes in for a consultation, they have usually decided what outcome to expect from their divorce.

If their expectations are positive, they generally believe the divorce will be settled fairly without much fuss. Because of that, they're likely to underestimate the size of the budget necessary to achieve their divorce goals. If they have a negative expectation of their divorce, they may overestimate the size of the budget necessary to achieve those goals. That may make them more inclined to settle, even if it's not in their best interests, as they generally believe that otherwise, the divorce will only be resolved with a divorce war.

I try to persuade spouses that they should not have *any* preconceived idea of how their divorce will go. The future is uncertain, and instead of trying to predict it, it's more productive to focus your energy on what you can control. What can you control? If you've been following along so far, you'll know that you have 100% control over:

- Choosing nondestructive responses to stress, pressure, and baiting
- Learning to *do nothing*
- Offering respect and understanding

You also have control over two other key factors:
- Your willingness to do what's necessary to prepare for the case
- Your attitude

Here's how to manage them.

Be willing to do your prep work before you're under the gun. With your attorney's guidance, you can roll up your sleeves and do the hard work of gathering the documentation that's necessary early in the process when you're least stressed, have the most energy, and can think best about the strategic aspects of the case. Although you may not enjoy spending time on your divorce unless there is a fire to put out, experience tells me that *waiting* to prepare will cause costly disruptions in your work and life schedule later. This also means that your delays will be bread and butter for most attorneys, who can bill needlessly to get unimportant things done urgently.

The goal is to reclaim your life. What will it take? A realistic attitude. To help my clients think in a constructive way about their divorce, I underline the basic point that they're in bad marriages that are ruining their lives. The goal of a divorce, I tell them, is to let you reclaim the life you *want* to live, and my job is to create a bridge to that life for you—a sane, realistic way forward built on positive attitudes and behavior. This approach works, because as the late business guru Stephen R. Covey put it, "You can't talk yourself out of a problem that you behaved yourself into." Early in the divorce process, I explain the stance spouses will need to take with a couple of analogies.

"I Only Have to Outrun You"

The first story I like to tell involves a married couple camping in the woods. As they're getting ready for bed in their tent, they hear some rustling outside. The wife peeks her head out and sees a bear lumbering toward their campsite. "It's a bear," she says, pulling on her clothes and running shoes while hustling out of the tent.

"Where are you going?" her husband says. "You can't outrun a bear!"

"I don't have to outrun the bear," the wife calls back as she sprints away. "I only have to outrun you!"

High-conflict divorce is a competition between two spouses where the court grades on a curve. Although you may feel you are not doing everything you can to get what you need in your divorce, just keep reminding yourself: you don't have to be perfect to get what you need—you just have to be better than your spouse.

Think of This as a Tennis Match

I also like to compare divorce litigation to a tennis match. Just because your spouse draws "first blood" and takes an early lead in the divorce by obtaining an early favorable ruling, it doesn't necessarily mean your needs will not be met in the divorce. Divorces are played out over an extended period, like a two-out-of-three-set tennis match (and sometimes three-out-of-five-set match). No matter what happens in the divorce, whether your spouse hires an aggressive attorney who is doing the shock-and-awe dance or they have a crafty old-timer attorney who piles on passive-aggressive challenges to wear you down in a war of attrition, the "winner" will ultimately prevail in a hard-fought contest that will be decided by only a few points either way.

If you understand that achieving your divorce goals will be a long, drawn-out, difficult process with many ups and downs and that you will likely suffer to achieve your goals, you're more likely to zero in on what's truly essential to you. Understanding this means that you will probably be more open to settlement earlier in the process—before you have overtaxed your budget. This strategy is often highly likely to produce the best-case scenario.

Managing Your Money Budget

First, understand that fairness can be expensive to come by. Most spouses come to a divorce wanting to spend the least amount possible to achieve their divorce goals. However, some of them find that they'll have to spend much more money than anticipated to obtain a fair and reasonable result. You already know that emotion-driven behavior can prolong a divorce and make costs balloon, but a number of factors peculiar to this process can also drive the cost higher on *both* sides. The two factors described below will give you a window into realities that many people wind up discovering only after they've been duped.

1. An Unscrupulous Attorney of the Nonmoneyed Spouse Can Milk the System

Divorce is a unique area of the law where it's presumed that the attorney fees of the "nonmoneyed" spouse will be paid at least in part by the spouse with more money. The law was designed to shield the nonmoneyed spouse against the bullying tactics of the wealthier one, but it is often used by certain attorneys as a sword. Usually, what happens in these situations is that the nonmoneyed spouse either borrows money or uses marital assets to pay for their attorney's retainer. Then, that attorney takes extreme (borderline frivolous) positions in an attempt to wear down the wealthier spouse.

There is no incentive for the nonmoneyed spouse's attorney to hold down costs because when attorneys apply to the court for their fees, most of them just put in requests for "estimated" amounts, such as $50,000 or $100,000, providing nothing more than a cursory description of how they will earn the money. Unfortunately, this is just the way the system works.

The court usually reduces the requested amount by 25% to 50% eventually. This is how the game is played. If the attorneys for the nonmoneyed spouse are less scrupulous, they will ramp up costs, knowing that they will most likely see only 50 cents on the dollar at best. Such tactics give all attorneys a bad name.

If you have exposure to fees because you're the moneyed spouse, try for "meaningful reallocation." If you're fortunate enough to obtain a wise judge (and remember that not all judges are wise, even though their black robes or gray hair can make them look that way), the way to prevent that kind of excessive billing is to ask the judge to make all fees for court-ordered expenses (such as expert fees) subject to reallocation. This means that even though the moneyed spouse may initially pay 90% or 100% of the cost of most orders, such as for the cost of a forensic mental health professional in a custody proceeding, the court may ultimately divide the cost differently between the parties, but only if there is a conclusion of the case after trial.

That last bit, "if there is a conclusion of the case after trial," is key, because, in truth, most courts never revisit the division of those costs after trial. Most cases settle before the trial ends, and the cost of the trial is so high that expenses paid during the litigation just get added on to the total divorce budget. However, in some cases, a court may divide the cost of these orders 50%-50%, subject to meaningful reallocation. In this scenario, the court will revisit these divisions of court-ordered expenses later in the case but *before* a trial, if necessary, to help the parties resolve their differences most efficiently when they are closer to settlement.

Meaningful reallocation gives the parties more equal financial responsibility during the litigation, even though their finances may be unequal. This appears unfair at first blush, but since the court is actually going to adjust the amount each side pays, the temporary burden the unmoneyed spouse bears is just another cost of the divorce litigation, like the retainer, for the parties to either negotiate or have the court decide.

Understanding the Divorce Budget

2. The Hours Your Attorney Is Billing You for Don't Necessarily Move the Case Forward

I focus on resolving cases either through negotiations or mediations (the carrot approach) or trial (the stick approach), and I have developed a reputation in my community for being an efficient, effective attorney. Many spouses find me through word of mouth at the start of the divorce process. Some, though, seek me out midstream because they've become frustrated with their first attorneys. Often, they are seeing attorney bills rise without any forward movement on their divorce. They may be particularly upset by what's called "block billing," where an associate (it's usually an associate) bills a block of time—say, 4 hours—and provides only a general description for the work, like "preparing statement of proposed disposition."

Some clients assume that the attorney is working hard on their behalf, but if they have been through trauma, which describes most people who go through a high-conflict divorce, their level of trust and faith is low. This low level of trust and faith can get projected onto their attorneys, whom they begin to see not as honorable advisors, but as hired guns. To make sure that your attorney is moving the ball forward, what I suggest you do is ask this simple question:

"What value, if any, does _____ (having three attorneys cc'd on an email, two attorneys at a court conference/settlement meeting) provide to us in helping us achieve our divorce goals?"

If the answer doesn't give you clarity or comfort, I suggest getting a second opinion from a trusted advisor.

(See Chapter 8 for a guide to determining when an attorney can be considered a trusted advisor and when you're dealing with a hired gun.)

Managing Your Energy Budget

Basic Principles: The big idea of the energy budget is that you need to maintain a reserve of physical and mental energy to sustain you through the divorce.

First, Lay Out an Actual Budget: You don't have infinite energy for your divorce, so playing the long game means conserving energy and using it only for getting the results you want.

Think in advance about the twists, turns, and challenges that you will face on your divorce journey. If you think only about where you want to end up without understanding the challenges you'll face, you'll only make your divorce that much more difficult. I'm not suggesting that you worry or catastrophize. Instead, stay flexible and know you'll need to keep devising and using strategies for handling the stress and negativity that are givens in a high-conflict divorce.

To start thinking about energy management, it is helpful to create an energy budget that factors in routines that will help you balance the energy you spend with positive routines for rebuilding.

To make that happen, you will need to do three things:

- Monitor your energy and spend it wisely in the moment, staying focused on your divorce goals in the present, and tending to them efficiently instead of procrastinating.

- Build physical energy reserves.
- Build emotional energy reserves.

Track Your Energy with the Hope Scale: You can monitor the status of your energy budget by using an imaginary energy scale that ranges from hopeful, which is an efficient use of energy, to anxious, which is not. Anxiety drains you physically and mentally, increasing your chances of not thinking clearly—which increases the odds that you will make decisions that may work against you. To keep yourself in a positive, hopeful state, at a minimum, you'll need to develop practices that keep you from giving up your energy to anxiety. Below are some of the most effective practices I know for building and conserving the energy you'll need to tackle the challenges ahead.

Build Physical Energy: I stress physical self-care to all my clients. Basics, like eating and sleeping well, can easily fall away in a high-conflict divorce, and many of my high-conflict divorce clients do not *regularly* take care of their physical health, but regular physical self-care is vital for the simple reason that your physical condition has a powerful effect on how you feel, and you'll need to feel as good as you can to make smarter decisions.

Day in and day out, be sure to pay attention to the following:

Scheduling Your Sleep: Our bodies need to reset at the end of the day, and stress skyrockets when that doesn't happen. Get the rest and reset you need by:

- Following Mr. Rogers' lead and going to bed at the same time each night.

- Getting more than 7 hours of sleep on most nights.
- Putting away smartphones and tablets at least an hour before going to bed.

Exercise: Cardio and yoga are good for relieving stress, a major energy drain in a high-conflict divorce. At minimum:

- Commit to at least 3 days a week of exercising during stressful times.
- Aim for 30 minutes of physical activity, but if you can't do 30 minutes, do 15 minutes. If you can't do 15 minutes, do 10 minutes. Exercising consistently 10 minutes a day is much better for your body than doing one hourlong class per week.

Nutrition: Bad nutrition wears you down. Aside from a weekly "cheat meal," consider following a healthy menu every day. I really cannot add any more to this subject other than what you can get from Mark Hyman, the *New York Times* best-selling health expert (see his book *Food: What the Heck Should I Eat?*), but here's my short answer to "What is good nutrition in a divorce?":

- Reduce Animal Protein, increase good fats (like those in olive oil, avocados, nuts, and salmon), and increase veggies.
- Decrease sugars and processed foods or ingredients that you cannot pronounce.

- Decrease coffee (one cup a day is okay).
- Decrease alcohol to no more than two glasses per week on weekends.

Build Emotional Energy: In addition to your physical energy, you'll need to focus on your mental energy—creating the right mind space. That can be more challenging to replenish, in at least some respects, than your physical energy, but here are a few practices that can help.

Journaling (aka: Free Therapy): Julia Cameron's *The Artist's Way* got me thinking about journaling in a whole new way. Because of her, I have regularly written in a journal for years now. Doing what she calls "the morning pages"—three pages of handwritten, stream-of-consciousness writing first thing in the morning—allows you to tap into your subconscious. Over time, this changes your perspective on issues that may be holding you back. It becomes easier to tap into your own wisdom and act on things you see yourself complaining about day after day.

Maybe you're like I was and think, "How can I possibly journal in the morning? I can barely do everything I need to as it is!" However, you'd probably find a way if I said to you, "I'll give you $100 if you get up 20 minutes earlier each day. If you get up 30 minutes earlier each day, I'll give you $1,000 just for waking up." Motivated by the value of the extra cash, you'd probably be willing to have a little less sleep.

I can't promise you extra *money* in exchange for putting in regular journaling time, but I can attest to the powerful clarity and emotional release that this practice will bring. Over time, the difference in your divorce and in your life will be priceless!

Visualizing (aka: Planning the Life You Want): This practice is a shortcut to your dreams, and it's especially good for people who, like some of my clients, do not fully believe they deserve or can have the life they want.

Here is how to do it. At least once a week, dedicate at least 15 minutes to thinking 5 years into the future. Imagine the life you want in movie-like detail. Where are you living? What are you doing? Who and what is around you?

Immerse yourself in a vision of that life, and then rewind the movie and travel back to the present, seeing all the things you'd have to do to achieve that goal. Imagine this reverse journey in as much movie-like detail as possible. Do you see your face in this visualization? How does it look? What color is the paint in your new apartment? What type of dog do you have, if you always wanted one? You get the idea!

When I did this, I saw myself as a writer, and my visualization practice made me realize that I was closer to my dream than I thought. I could put the writing I do as an attorney in a new context and see it as an important step in the process. The same sort of thing happens for many of my clients. They can see not just their futures, but their current lives in an inspiring light. Their dreams seem possible and within reach. After visualizing about writing and other dreams, I will say that doing this really does work. If you want to have the life you want, start visualizing now. If you'd like to try it, Googling Maxwell

Maltz or *The Success Principles* will point you in the right direction.

Mind Settling (aka Meditation): A mind-settling practice can help you put space between a stimulus and a response so that you won't be so reactive. It's also designed to reset the mind. Starting a practice can be daunting, but the rewards are tremendous. An easy way to start is through guided sessions (there are plenty of free meditation apps and YouTube videos to get you started). Don't get too hung up about how long you give your mind to settle. If you're new to the idea, start with 1-3 minutes every day. When you can do that comfortably, increase the time. I would rather see you do 3 minutes every day than 10 minutes 2 days a week. The idea is to develop a consistent practice. It will change you energetically, and that will change the nature of any conflict you are in.

Managing Your Time Budget

Value your time: A high-conflict divorce can take years to resolve. Once you reach just *that* resolution, you may wind up in a cold war with your ex that lasts for decades. Knowing this, it makes sense to guard your precious time as much as possible. Time is not renewable but is invaluable. It is very hard not to overtax your time budget as you go through your divorce. There is much to do in order to properly prepare, and even if you are highly efficient and have a supremely efficient attorney, you'll still be asked to put in hours that may seem difficult to find, but you can likely be more efficient than you think, if you use the following practices.

Always have an agenda: I get many requests to sit down for a four-way or settlement meeting with counsel and clients to try to resolve the divorce. Early in my career I would always attend these settlement meetings, but I have learned that unless there is an agreed-upon agenda, not much will happen there except incurring legal fees. Even if you have an agenda, there is no guarantee that the attorneys will follow it. I suggest putting a strict time limit on meetings and following a rigid agenda. If you feel the other side will overpower you or play games, consider using a mediator for a five-way meeting, which would include counsel and the clients.

Hold fast to the practice of not responding for at least 24 hours: If you are triggered even a little by your spouse's texts or emails, instead of unleashing a tirade, put down the phone, close your email window, and do not respond for at least 24 hours. When and if you do respond—and remember that the wisest choice is often to do nothing—I advise against asking your attorney to write your emails or texts for you, though in the beginning, it may be helpful to have them (or a divorce coach) give you a model for how to respond to conflict in a way that's useful and consistent. You need to start developing the skills necessary for better communication under pressure, even if the other side engages in bad communication. If you need extra help in crafting better communications to your spouse, a good resource to use is the popular BIFF statements from master mediator Bill Eddy. He teaches you how to write communications that are brief, informative, friendly, and firm.

Ask your lawyer not to forward Friday emails from opposing attorneys: A particular type of attorney deliberately sends aggressive settlement letters or other demands on Friday afternoon. Naively, thinking I was being a good attorney, I used to forward those messages to my clients. I learned the hard way that that was just what the other side wanted me to do (controlling the frame!). They want you, the opposing client, to have all weekend to stew, become irrational, and overreact—it weakens you and makes their job easier. I am chagrined to say that it took me years to realize this, and as soon as I did, I stopped those Friday forwards.

Now if I receive a late-Friday message from opposing counsel, I hold on to it until Monday. If I feel triggered by the content, I usually wait at least a week so I can send my client not just the opposing counsel's message, but also a copy of my written response to it, along with a video explaining my thinking on their missive and my response. This lets my clients see things more holistically rather than being driven by their gut reaction and emotions. If your attorney is still caught up in forwarding emails from opposing counsel on Fridays, please tell them to stop. Everyone will be calmer, and by *not* dealing with opposing counsel over the weekend, you can get much-needed renewal and rest.

Resist the time bullies: Another technique super-aggressive attorneys use to manipulate time is to give you the impression of urgency when none exists. I call this tactic "time-bullying." They want you to enter into handwritten agreements (or stipulations) in court that do not give you or your attorney time to fully think through issues. They send versions of agreements a day or two before a self-imposed deadline that does not give you time to meet with your attorney and discuss these issues in anything other than a pressurized way.

My suggestion is that you refrain from signing any agreements that you do not feel you have had a full opportunity to think through—especially if they involve your children—even if this means making you unpopular with the other side, or taking heat from the court. If your attorney does not have a concern about the agreement but you do, I would suggest that you still consider waiting or getting a second opinion to make sure what your attorney advises is correct.

KEY POINTS: Understanding the Divorce Budget

- No one has an unlimited amount of time, energy, money, and emotion to cover their divorce. Even if you have an unlimited financial budget, you might not have an unlimited budget of time or energy.

- You will need to start thinking about conserving your divorce resources for what is likely to be a marathon, not a sprint.

- The other side will make many attempts to use up your budget early in the process so you will not have any resources left for the real battles ahead. That means you need to stay super efficient with your budget if you are going to give yourself a fair chance of succeeding.

- If you manage your divorce budget properly, you will have enough in your tank to finish stronger than your spouse, who will likely be well over budget by the end of the process.

- *Remember:* The smart strategy is not about taking a first-strike lead to win your divorce. Focus simply on crossing that finish line ahead of your spouse.

Chapter 6.
Learn Divorce Attorney Tactics

When you're involved in a high-conflict divorce, it can feel as though you've been thrown into a boxing ring with an opponent you need to defend yourself against and must defeat at all costs. The problem is that at first—and even well into the process—you may not understand the art of the fight, the strategies that are being used against you, and what kinds of strategies might be most effective to use against the other party.

I'd like to break down a few basic styles and tactics that I commonly see and coach you regarding the process and how to respond. If you aren't familiar with these tactics, you'll likely take them personally instead of thinking about your long-term divorce goals, and you may wind up being preoccupied with defending yourself within a frame that was created by the other side, which may have no bearing on the central issues in your divorce, nor may it even be true. These fundamentals won't turn you into your own lawyer, but they'll help you see what's happening, what's important, and what you need to do to stay sane and effective.

Approaches to Resolving a Divorce

Lawyers use three different ways of approaching a divorce:

The collaborative model looks for everyone to win.

The diplomatic model similarly wants everyone to win, but realizes that a diplomat may have to suffer short-term losses for long-term gains.

However, if you're in a high-conflict divorce, those aren't the styles that are in play. Instead, you're facing **the competitive, win-at-all-costs model,** a fight to the death of the relationship in which you're likely to incur damage beyond repair. The tactics are aggressive, compromise is a last resort, and the fighting may be—or seem to be—petty and underhanded. You'll need to stay level-headed and remember that your attorney is like a boxing trainer who's helping you prepare for your day in court—the day you actually step into the box for cross-examination. The attorney cannot help you on cross, but he or she can prepare you and help you conserve your energy and maintain your focus, ensuring that you have not wasted time, money, or emotional reserves on diversions that won't help you win.

Just as in boxing, divorce cases are won and lost primarily in the mind. The client who wins may not be the strongest, but he or she will always be the one who is smarter in executing certain tactics that increase the probability of success.

If you want to win, these are the four primary attorneys' tactics you'll need to understand and know how to counter.

Tactic 1: The Swarmer (aka: The Pressure Cooker)

A divorce attorney who's a Swarmer applies constant pressure. Swarmers believe that the best defense is a good offense. Their offense of choice is "death by a thousand cuts." Not only will a Swarmer try to slowly impeach your credibility by raising every imaginable issue to the judge, but the Swarmer will also fight everything in an effort to overwhelm you.

Learn Divorce Attorney Tactics

If you're a dad fighting for custody, the Swarmer might raise issues such as "He let the 6-year-old cross the street by herself," or "He was late two times last week picking the child up from daycare," adding a new grievance every time you turn around.

At the same time, Swarmers fight off compromises. If you ask a judge to award you child support from your child's mother, the Swarmer will make a motion to claim that she needs you to pay for "extra childcare now that she has to work harder to make more money to support the children."

The Swarmer's goal: The Swarmer will ask for the sun, moon, and stars, beat you up for years over nonissues, force you to needlessly spend money on litigation over those nonissues—and bill for a lot of time in the process.

The Swarmer's endgame: The Swarmer keeps litigation dragging on but doesn't actually have a case. Those thousand paper-cut issues do not add up to a victory for your ex, so after collecting large fees for the case, the Swarmer eventually settles at a reasonable (or almost reasonable) level if they haven't exhausted you first and made you give in.

What the Swarmer doesn't want you to know: The Swarmer strategy is strong evidence that your case is persuasive. The Swarmer is focused on the time the 6-year-old crossed the street without supervision because the Swarmer does not have anything better to focus on, while you and your attorney may have a knockout punch or two.

How to Win against a Swarmer

1. Don't take the bait. Don't respond to everything the Swarmer throws at you. In fact, you probably will want to respond to very little of it. Many of the attempted "cuts" will come in emails and letters. Remember that the court is not aware of any of it (or at least not focused on it) until it comes in the form of a motion or is discussed at a court conference.

2. Don't sweat the small stuff. Ask your attorney this key question: On a scale of 1 to 10, how relevant is this to the main issue of our case? If it's under a 4, don't react at all. If it's a 4, 5, or 6, wait to see if it'll turn into anything. Take notes and keep a journal tracking how serious the Swarmer seems to be about the issue. Naturally, the Swarmer is going to try to inflate the importance of the issues but they might be just red herrings, so be careful.

3. Know why you're responding. Ask your lawyer: Do I need to use my budget (time/money/energy/emotion) to respond to this issue?

4. Stay on point. Know your argument and stick to it. Don't let the Swarmer distract and overwhelm you with nonsense. Be like a politician with talking points that you keep steering the discussion back to. It may feel good to fire off a response to the latest insult or jab, but if you do it, you're playing into the Swarmer's strategy by giving energy to *their* arguments. Step out of the way, return the focus to your own argument, and let the Swarmer punch away at air.

Tactic 2: The Brawler (Going for a One-Punch Knockout)

Brawlers, unlike Swarmers, have more than "paper cut" jabs—they are armed with issues that can knock you out with a one-punch. They know or imply you're a workaholic who's always out of the country, trying to get sole custody, while the other parent works from home and could pay more attention to the child. They might reveal that you were having affairs and making the kids complicit or had an addiction problem, a criminal history, or financial entanglements.

It takes elite-level defense to face off with Brawlers, and getting that level of defense has as much to do with you as with your lawyer.

The Brawler's goal: The Brawler tries to set a trap (the knockout punch) that's hard for you to recover from, even if the trap is not directly related to the contested issues before the court.

The Brawler's endgame: To have you agree to your spouse's demands through fear and shame tactics.

What the Brawler doesn't want you to know: If the Brawler has the goods on you regarding an issue that's directly related to the contested issues before the court, such as that you're not paying your share of education expenses but want to be the primary custodial parent, you'd be wise to think about settlement options early in the process instead of incurring expenses for a fight you're likely to lose.

However, if the Brawler has the goods on you concerning an incident or topic that's only indirectly related to the contested issues before the court (our polarizing political views), then the case is really all about reframing the issues before the court so that it's more persuaded by the *real* issues of the divorce rather than the distraction of a character assassination sideshow.

How You Win against a Brawler

1. Come clean with your lawyer immediately about any strong weaknesses. Many clients find it hard to admit the truth early in a litigation, but it's essential. Write a long message to your attorney (uploaded to a client portal for security reasons, not sent through Gmail) and then sit down with them a week later and really tell them the truth. If you don't, there's a strong probability you'll get destroyed later on—and also have to pay the other side's attorney fees.

2. Give your attorney any case-ending leverage you have against your ex. Maybe you're a workaholic, but your spouse is a cocaine addict or views child sex abuse images. Be sure your attorney knows what you know.

3. Don't make up allegations. The "you'll get destroyed and pay the other side's legal fees" cautions apply here too.

4. If you've got the goods, fight back. Brawlers may depend too heavily on knock out punches. If you are 100% sure that the allegations the other side is making against you are nonsense, then your attorney will be able to duck, weave, and cover as the Brawler takes aim during trial, neutralizing attempts to weaken your credibility.

5. *Stay on point.* When you're dealing with a Brawler, knowing your argument and sticking to it is the only way to win.

Tactic 3: The Boxer (Winning on Points)

Every fight is not a knockout. A particular breed of attorney, the class act I call the Boxer, seems to adhere to the legal equivalent of the Hippocratic Oath: "first, do no harm." Boxers focus not on tearing the other side down with a barrage of small issues or looking for that one-punch knockout, but on building an airtight defense.

They can bob and weave so well it's hard to hit them where it hurts. Elite levels of this form use devastating counterpunching as their offense by creating a counter theme that is as strong as any offense the opposing attorney may lob your way.

Boxer attorneys are both patient and quick, waiting for openings and then striking. They can ride out attacks and have the self-control to use aggression only when it's measured and appropriate.

The Boxer's goal: Efficient resolution of divorces using only as much of the budget (time, energy, money, emotion) as necessary to achieve goals that are important to a client's long-term postdivorce life. This is the attorney you most want on your team as you face the resource-depleting tactics of Swarmers and Brawlers, or the intimidation of a Top Dog (see next category).

The Boxer's endgame: Helping clients move on with their lives without having unnecessary battle scars or budget-busting divorces.

What the Boxer doesn't want you to know: That they're more interested in winning than impressing someone (even you) with razzle-dazzle. Since Boxers are primarily focused on defense, theirs is not a flashy style to observe. You may want your Boxer-type attorney to be more aggressive (throw more punches) because you believe that that's how you win the divorce game, but the Boxer is a strategist who packs energy into select moves that can damage the other side and doesn't waste resources on an ineffective barrage of activity.

If you have a Boxer type of attorney, and you think you want a more aggressive style, have a talk about tactics and strategy, and be sure you understand what's behind the calculated response you're seeing. Be very clear about the likely costs of letting go of this trusted advisor. The Boxer will keep you focused on what's in your control and on getting results, not on meaningless hits of ego gratification or revenge.

How You Win against a Boxer

1. Know that Boxers are likely not building to an earth-shattering moment that destroys your credibility. Their real goal is to win more arguments on balance than you do, so that when the court balances all the factors, the probabilities favor them, not you.

2. Work to control the narrative. For example, if they try to win a high level of child support by claiming that you use your business to pay for big-ticket personal expenses, don't get sucked in and become single focused on defending yourself. Instead, change the narrative to offense, and hit them with a counterpunch of "The father is underemployed—and is actually trying to use child support as spousal support." Now you have a real fight, and when the dust clears you will be ahead on points if your attorney is skillful and prepared enough.

3. Stay on point. Remember that the way to keep a Boxer from winning on points is to win on points yourself, giving the court reasons to support you that don't hinge on "I didn't do what the other guy said." Stay focused on the points *you* want to make, not the ones the other side is dictating.

Tactic 4: The Top Dog (Unleashing the Mutant Beasts)

Top Dogs are expensive ($1,000+ an hour in NYC in 2022), elite attorneys who have the defensive capability of the Boxer coupled with the punching power of the Brawler and the Swarmer's ability to apply unrelenting pressure. These attorneys are usually named partners with several associates. Lawyering as big business is the name of the game with these toughies.

If your spouse hired a Top Dog, you and your divorce attorney are in for a real test. The only way to beat this type of attorney—and yes, it can be done—is to hire an elite counterpuncher (the most skillful of Boxers). This case will not end early unless the Top Dog is distracted by other larger cases in their office. Top Dogs will not be your best friend. They will either be rude and obnoxious or coolly distant and super professional. They will work to control the momentum of the divorce. However, you can slow them down if you make them pay every time they try to hurt you.

If the courtroom fight is between two Top Dogs, yours and theirs, be prepared for one of two scenarios. There's an off chance of a quick settlement in which each side names a figure to wrap things up quickly, but most likely, you'll be facing a pointless 12-round battle in which the evenly matched dogs earn gold-plated fees, and no one really gets hurt in the end—professional courtesy. Unless you relish the thought of prolonged, top-dollar litigation, hiring an elite Boxer is the best way to face off with a Top Dog.

The Top Dog's goal: Make easy things difficult in order to increase the budget (time, energy, emotion, money) and decrease the other side's willingness to engage with them.

The Top Dog's endgame: The Top Dog's goal is to achieve the client's objectives even if the "cost" of achieving them outweighs the "benefit."

What the Top Dog doesn't want you to know: Top Dogs lose interest quickly if the "meal" is uninspiring, so even if your spouse hired a Top Dog as their attorney, unless your divorce is one of the biggest cases in the office, your spouse will be primarily represented by a pale version of the Top Dog, such as a midtier associate. That person may *believe* that they are Top Dog by proxy, but as any back-up singer knows, standing 20 feet from a star does not mean you have achieved stardom. In effect, your spouse has been seduced into a budget-busting divorce without even understanding that once the retainer is signed, face time with the Top Dog will be infrequent at best. You have more power than you think in this scenario; the pseudo–Top Dog is generally an easy match for a Boxer.

Even if the Top Dog is in beast mode, focused on its "prey" (you), you could still avoid a mauling if you have retained a highly competent attorney, your Boxer. You and your attorney will have to roll up your sleeves and do the work that's necessary (the Three Ps: prepare, prepare, prepare) for upcoming battles so that when the time comes, you will have armed yourself with the weapons necessary to survive, if not thrive.

How You Win against a Top Dog:

1. Respond strategically, not reflexively. Ignore about 95% of what they say but have at the ready three to five powerful comebacks every time they try to inflict pain at conferences by hurting your credibility. Hurt theirs too.

2. Make your moves when the Top Dog is muzzled. This happens two times in the divorce: during the deposition and during the cross-examination.

3. Show that you can hurt the Top Dog's client at the deposition. If you can do this, the Top Dog may be willing to back off from unreasonable positions and thus shorten your litigation.

4. Use expert counterpunching on cross-examination. This is the hard way of winning, but it can be done, especially if you give your lawyer an edge in two simple ways:

- Order real-time or daily transcripts. The days of your divorce attorney having tons of trial experience are mostly over, so if you aren't fortunate enough to have hired a trial whiz, ordering real-time or daily transcripts gives your attorney a fighting chance to do some damage during cross-examination. Your attorney will be super prepared and have the potential to bring real firepower into the cross-examination, since it's possible to use the other side's *exact words* against them.

- Have an extra set of ears at trial, not necessarily another sophisticated attorney, but a paralegal who may hear things you or your attorney cannot.

Even having a general understanding of these tactics and the basic ways of responding to them will help you stay focused. Anytime you feel overpowered, remember: the spouse who's the smartest, sanest, and most strategic is very likely to win. And that spouse can be *you*.

KEY POINTS: Learn Divorce Attorney Tactics

Be prepared to face four different kinds of attorneys using four common tactics.

- The Swarmer applies constant pressure on issues that are mostly unimportant and not urgent issues, though they make them seem so.

- The Brawler is different from the Swarmer in that the pressure that they're focused on is case-ending. You need to come clean with your attorney to make sure that the case-ending evidence will not come out later in the process, such as on the witness stand, after you've exhausted your budget and hoped the Brawler wouldn't go there.

- The Boxer primarily believes that creative problem solving is better than scare tactics in resolving divorces. The Boxer's defense is so good that it's hard to hurt them. If you do start poking at them, their "counterpunches" will be so effective that they're as strong as any offense that you've lobbed their way.

- Top Dogs are expensive, high-powered attorneys who have the defensive capability of the Boxer coupled with the punching power of the Brawler and the Swarmer's ability to apply unrelenting pressure. The name of the game with these toughies is to work on the most profitable cases possible.

For guidance on how to find the best attorney for you and your situation, see Chapter 8.

Chapter 7.
Accept that the Court Is Always Right

Divorces are usually tried before a judge, not a jury. Judges are human! Like you and me, they have their own biases and learning styles. In fact, you can try the exact same case before ten different judges and get that many different results.

You can't know exactly how big your divorce budget will need to be. But you can get a good preview of the expenses to come early on by looking objectively and subjectively at how the judge presiding over your divorce will likely view the issues of your divorce. Your attorney will most likely know if the judge is biased against stay-at-home parents of school-age children. The attorney will also know if the judge supports equal or almost equal parenting time or is more traditional in their parenting views. Taking this information seriously will help you steer clear of a budget-busting trial.

Every Judge's Goal: To Get You to Settle Instead of Going to Trial

Divorce courts are crowded with cases, and those that go to trial tax everyone's resources—the spouses', the children's, and the court's. For that reason, attorneys and judges use a variety of tools to push divorcing couples toward settlement.

The Court Conference

If your divorce cannot be settled through negotiations, usually one of the attorneys will schedule a court conference. Most divorces are settled at these conferences, where the parties' attorneys update the judge on which issues have and haven't been resolved. The conferences give the litigants the feeling that they had "their day in court," and the settlements reached there let the court manage its docket, as court conferences are much less taxing on the court than trials.

Parties Required to Appear

A unique feature of divorce litigation is that in many jurisdictions, parties are *required* to appear with their attorneys at all court conferences. (In most types of litigation, the attorneys appear on behalf of their clients at all pretrial conferences.)

Having to appear at all court conferences automatically increases your divorce budget, because you'll have to take time away from your personal and professional life to come to court, which is a place most people are uncomfortable attending. You may face resistance at work when you ask for time off to make your court appearances. In fact, I have had clients who were put on probation by their employers and even fired because court dates interfered so much with their jobs. You may also have to arrange childcare, even if the other spouse refuses to pay for it and you don't have the funds to cover it yourself.

The pressure all this will put you under is intentional. The system is designed to tax your divorce budget early on, to give you the incentive to resolve your case well before trial.

Advisory Opinions

The judge has another way to encourage you to keep from going to trial. After hearing about the issues in your case, she or he may be willing to give you an "advisory" opinion about how it should be resolved. These advisory opinions are, of course, not binding. Instead, they come with the weight of the court behind them and make most litigants feel that the judge has heard their concerns.

Not every judge will give an advisory opinion; I've observed that the busier the courtroom, the more willing the court is to offer one. With the guidance from the court received at the initial conferences, most litigants can resolve their divorces satisfactorily *under the circumstances*—that is, given the preferences of this judge in this case.

Still, some litigants feel so strongly about their positions that they are willing to double down and continue to increase their budget with discovery and trial preparations either to force the other side's hand (divorce litigation is also a mind game) or to prove themselves right, because they really believe their position should prevail at trial.

However, an advisory opinion can change the calculus. One of my clients wanted a quick and fair divorce after a long, unhappy marriage to a successful businessman. The other side wanted to give my client a very low spousal support award for a very short period of time. However, they backed off that position when the court's advisory opinion indicated that those terms weren't likely to fly. If not for that, we would not have been able to resolve the divorce on terms my client found satisfactory in such a short period of time.

Making the Most of the Opinion: Let Your Attorney Coach You

If you are lucky enough to receive an advisory opinion in your divorce, it's wise to take advantage of it. The best divorce attorneys shine when using an advisory opinion to manage their clients' expectations and budgets. These attorneys are not only effective advocates and competent trial lawyers, but also first-class counselors of the law—in other words, coaches who can convey the court's thinking and the most productive way of working within it. (Remember: the court is always right!)

By being a first-class counselor—aka: your coach—your divorce attorney is helping you make the best decision in the thick of emotional stress, at a time when it's extremely difficult to be thinking at your best. His or her goal is to help you understand the likely direction of the case and also to show you how the judge has heard and understood your concerns. Once you can see both of those things, it's easier to come off your stated position and make the compromises that will allow you to settle the case in a way that lines up with the court's direction and your divorce goals.

Warnings and Pretrial Conferences

When divorce attorneys are unable to persuade their clients of the benefits of heeding the court's advisory opin-

Accept that the Court Is Always Right

ion, the court may step in and attempt to dissuade the parties from proceeding with litigation through various tactics, such as focusing on the risks involved in litigation. The court will warn you of the uncertainty, the high costs, and the time-intensive challenges ahead. It may also schedule several pretrial conferences just to pressure you further to settle your divorce.

If those tactics don't work and you remain undeterred by the adversity you're facing not only from the other side, but also from the court (and the system, which is set up to settle cases), the case will *ultimately* proceed to trial. It is important to note that the trial will likely be many times as long and twice as expensive as budgeted for. It is also important to note that in busier courts, such as the courts of New York City, *years* can elapse between commencing a divorce case and getting a written decision after trial!

Fight Bad Decisions with Do-Overs

Though the court is always right, it may fall for tactics designed to muddy the waters and work against you—simply because its members are human. Divorce attorneys have to be very creative in attempting to persuade the court. For example, if the facts are overwhelmingly against their client they may feel compelled to create a diversion, a legal trojan horse if you will, designed for the sole purpose of distracting the court from the real issues of the case.

For example, if Ryan is the primary parent of a young child, his spouse's attorney may allege that he is inappropriate with the child because he bathes with him—even though Ryan and his spouse always bathed naked together with the child. So at every court conference, the only issue that will be raised is how inappropriate Ryan is with the child. If his attorney is not able to create a counter theme—for instance that the mother is focusing on this point in order to distract from the fact that she's a cocaine addict—then the court maybe influenced by this trojan horse and not render an equitable decision. It may, for instance, limit Ryan to supervised visits with the child he's been caring for almost single-handedly.

If you've got an unlimited budget, you can always appeal a bad decision and start the process over again. Most spouses, however, do not have such a budget. My suggestion then is to strongly consider having your attorney make a *motion for reconsideration* (sometimes called reargument). The cost of doing this motion is much less than taking an appeal, and the odds of winning your motion, versus winning on an appeal, are much greater. Here's a look at how each of these options works.

Second Chances, aka: Motions to Reconsider

One way to right a court wrong is to ask for a motion to renew, reconsider, or reargue. It involves making an application to the judge to have the court look over issues of fact or law that, if they were included in the original decision, would make the court rule in your favor. In essence, you're pointing out laws or details that you brought up earlier and saying "Please look at these factors again." I would say your odds of getting relief on such a motion are about 50%.

Accept that the Court Is Always Right

PROS

- Relatively efficient use of budget
- Relatively fast compared to an appeal
- Judge is fully familiar with the case
- Getting at least some of what you are requesting

CONS

- Any bias the judge had still remains.
- A motion to renew, reconsider, or reargue is not a complete review of the issues presented (we call that a "de novo review"); it is more limited in scope. In using a motion like this, you waive your right to raise new issues and can only have the court look at points you've already made. This means that if you forgot something important originally, you won't be allowed to add it now.

Asking for a Complete Do-Over: The Appeal

If you want a full review of the facts and law by a new judge, what you'll have to do in most situations is to take an appeal. This is a high-cost option in which the odds of winning are extremely long. Only 5% of cases that go to trial are tried to completion because 95% of people settle before they get there. Of the 5% who go all the way through the process, only 25% or so take an appeal—that's a little more than 1% of cases. And I'd say that those people have less than a 25% chance of winning.

Winning on appeal does happen, of course. Think of all the court proceedings same-sex couples had to go through for the courts to recognize their right to marry.

If you have that kind of resolve and belief in your position, then you should think about creating an appeal budget early in the divorce process if things are not going your way. Sometimes it really is wiser to use your limited resources where they can make the most difference, and in some special cases, that may be during an appeal.

PROS

- Full review of the record
- New perspective from multiple justices
- Can bring up new legal theories not raised before, which you may not be able to raise in the do-over approach

CONS

- Expensive!
- Low odds of winning

KEY POINTS: Accept that the Court Is Always Right

- Attorneys control the courtroom in the beginning of the divorce process, not the judge.
- Attorneys move your case through the court system, but the court has the ultimate responsibility to act as the decision maker in your divorce.
- Most spouses settle because they don't want to give this control to the court.
- If you do have to proceed to a decision, that decision may not go your way. In such moments, remember two critical rules. Rule 1: the court is always right. Rule 2: when the court is wrong, see Rule 1.
- If the court decides against you, all hope is not lost. You can request a reconsideration of the court's decision. Think of a reconsideration as a mini-appeal, which is much cheaper than a full-blown appeal. It will give you much greater odds of persuading the judge that he or she may have overlooked the facts or law, which caused them to rule against you.

Chapter 8.
How to Find the Best Attorney for You

It can be hard to think clearly about finding the right divorce attorney to guide you through the maze of decisions you'll need to make as you end your marriage and start a new life.

Many people seeking a divorce have bad feelings toward their spouse, and these feelings cloud their thinking and the choices they make in their divorce.

URGENCY, ANGER, AND FEAR can drive decision-making, and most people just take the path of least resistance—hiring the best attorney they can afford and hoping that things go their way.

Unfortunately, that lack of strategy doesn't always go well.

In my practice, I have taken over many cases for clients who were seduced by the pricey "Top Dog" attorneys, thinking they'd get maximum efficiency and firepower against their spouse by paying top dollar. What they found was that their divorce was not ending as quickly as they expected and that as time went on, their marquee-name attorney was no longer representing their best interests, because he or she was distracted or had pawned them off to an associate who, although better priced, wasn't proving to be as effective as they needed.

On the other end of the spectrum, I have worked with many people who stepped into their divorce overconfidently, believing that they had a simple uncontested divorce. These people believed there was no need to invest their resources (time, energy, emotion, money) in the process unless things went awry. They didn't see the need to be tactical in how they approached the divorce, so they didn't think through the implications of their decisions as they went along. For instance, they didn't speak with an attorney before moving out of the marital home even though they wanted primary custody of the children, not realizing that the move could negatively impact their legal positions if things went south.

If you have children or give/receive support, you'll need an attorney. You may be able to manage decision-making on your own and take a wait-and-see approach to finding legal counsel if you can make a "walk away" (a clean break in your divorce). However, if you still have postdivorce issues to work out, such as sharing children or financial-support obligations, then as much as you want to "cut bait and run," doing that may hurt you in the long term.

The decisions you make now—such things as where you live, what you say to your spouse, and how you handle your children—could impact your divorce and postdivorce life. You need guidance, and you need to make sure that you're hiring the right type of attorney for *you*.

I say *for you* because the attorney-client relationship is a very personal one. You most likely will reveal things to your attorney that you might not even tell your best friends—your dark secrets, the intimate details of your finances, and much more. You have to feel comfortable doing that, which is why there is no one-size-fits-all approach to choosing a divorce lawyer.

I'd like to share a couple of basic guidelines based on what I've seen in my 20-year career: in a difficult divorce, I'd strongly advise you to consider hiring a trusted advisor over an expert for hire and to choose a wise dog of an attorney over a bulldog divorce attorney. Let me explain what I mean.

Expert for Hire vs. Trusted Advisor

You want an attorney to give you advice that's in your best interests, which means that the advice is both sound and affordable for you. Expert-for-hire attorneys, on the other hand, aren't motivated by affordability. Given a choice between a simple, efficient solution to your problem and one that will eat up court and preparation time, the guns for hire will choose the one that runs up the clock so they'll make more money.

This is common because the system is set up to reward selling *time,* which can be given a specific value, but it doesn't necessarily reward providing good advice, which may be priceless. Fortunately, there are also skilled attorneys who will put you first, look past their own financial self-interests, and tell you the truth, unvarnished.

How do you recognize those trusted advisors? By the questions they ask and in the direct manner in which they talk with you about your priorities, your tolerance for risk, and your divorce budget—how much time, money, energy, and emotion you're willing and able to invest in your divorce. They'll talk to you directly about the costs, risks, and trade-offs involved in the choices they offer you, and they'll show you that they know what's most important to you.

Trusted advisors truly get to know you, learn about your interests, goals, and personality, and use their legal expertise and personal understanding of your unique situation to give you the best solutions to your problems based on your risk tolerance and budget.

These attorneys are as astute, kind, and clever as the waiter who sees two poor college sweethearts come into his restaurant—the most expensive one in town—to celebrate an important milestone (third date, ha!). Recognizing that they don't necessarily have the money for the experience, he tells them: "The chef is so honored that you've chosen our restaurant for your night out that she wants to cook you the same meal she gives the people closest to her, if you'll allow her the honor." The price for the two of them, the waiter adds, will be $40 including wine, which is not even the price of one of the entrees at the restaurant.

The college couple revels in the special treatment and enjoys their dinner in the restaurant's amazing ambiance, not knowing that their feast was the same one given to the restaurant staff earlier in the day.

The astute waiter and chef have "lost money on the deal," but with their kind, resourceful solution, they have created clients for life.

That's the human, long-term perspective they share with trusted advisors.

Bulldog vs. Wise Dog

When the media portrays the best divorce attorney to retain, I often hear talk about stereotypical "tough guys"—

the sharks, the barracudas, the pit bulls. When you face them in your divorce, those are the lawyers who pile on aggressive, high-pressure tactics from the get-go, fighting every issue, compromising on nothing, working to pulverize your credibility, all so you'll just cave in and agree to a settlement that gives them everything they want (which is *everything*).

I often go up against this type of attorney, and if a divorce is resolved in the first phase, before the rule of law imposes its will, I would agree that their "shock and awe" approach to litigation gives them a distinct advantage—it scares most people into submission.

But—and here is the big but—divorce cases have two phases. If you can weather the shock-and-awe storm, a judge resolves your divorce, and when this happens, I would bet on a wise dog of an attorney any day of the week. The reason is simple: they do only what's necessary to get the job done.

To see what I'm talking about, think about the 2017 boxing match between a bulldog mixed martial artist—Conor McGregor, arguably one of the best MMA fighters of all time—and a wise-dog boxer, Floyd Mayweather Jr., arguably one of the best boxers of all time.

In the first phase of that boxing match, if you include all of the publicity, promotion, and first few rounds of the fight, it's fair to say that bulldog Conor McGregor "won" with his shock-and-awe theatrics.

However, as in a divorce, there was a second phase to that boxing contest. McGregor had counted on his prematch bravado and bullying to faze and cripple Mayweather early on for an easy knock-out, so he spent all his energy there. Eventually, he realized to his dismay that to win, he'd have to go the distance with Mayweather. He wasn't prepared for that, and Mayweather calmly outboxed him in the second phase to take the contest.

This is what happens in most of my cases. The other spouse hires a name-brand, aggressive bulldog of an attorney who believes that my client will cave based on a shock-and-awe approach to litigation, and when that doesn't work, we move to phase two of the proceedings. This is no fun for the other spouse, who is paying top dollar to the bulldog and has racked up a towering pile of bills for a failed strategy. Now the spouse gets more reasonable, which allows me to calmly bargain for and get what my client needs. My ego would like to sometimes repay the bulldog in kind for the bruising first round of attacks by being nasty, brash, and aggressive, but experience tells me that the best attorneys are classy, tactical, and shrewd. They're wise dogs.

What separates winners in a difficult divorce is just a few points here or there, and you're giving yourself the best chances of doing that if you and your attorney can be composed. That's why you want the wise-dog attorney. When the wise dog is your trusted advisor, you're in very good hands.

How to Find the Best Attorney for You

- You want an attorney to give you advice that's in your best interests, not a gun for hire that will choose a strategy that runs up the clock so they'll make more money.

- If you can weather the shock-and-awe storm of a bulldog attorney, a judge resolves your divorce, and when this happens, I would bet on a wise dog of an attorney any day of the week. The reason is simple: they do only what's necessary to get the job done.

Chapter 9.
Becoming Persuasive

Learning to deescalate disagreements before they turn into conflicts takes patience and practice. You'll have to consciously pause some of your deepest instincts and ignore the feeling that you're headed in the wrong direction, but it's the only way to get what you need and want in your divorce. Because this new way of behaving is so important, I'd like to give you a chance to practice so that you can develop a mindset that will help you stay committed to using deescalation as the foundation for dealing with your spouse.

I showed you in Chapter 4 how to become less defensive. Here's a mini-guide to turning nondefensiveness to persuasion, and a look at how one of my clients used a non-defensive stance to persuade her spouse to think with her to solve a sticky problem.

HERE'S A LITTLE SECRET about human psychology that unlocks the art of persuasion: no matter what people say they want, most of the time, what they actually want isn't the thing or concession itself. They want the *feeling* that it represents, so if you can dig deep to understand the need they're trying to satisfy (such as a need for respect, consideration, freedom, or peace), you can actually give them what they want—and make them feel as though they've won something important from you—without giving them what they asked for.

That immediately changes the terms and tone of the conversation and creates an opening for you (and maybe your spouse) to imagine possibilities beyond the standoff on the table. I described this in the defensiveness chapter in terms of looking for shared values, but for some people, things click more easily when we talk about *identifying the feeling*, so let's do that here.

Getting to the Feeling Level

The feeling behind your spouse's request is everything, and you get to it by asking: What's the *positive* need my spouse is trying to meet (or offer to our child) in this situation? Once you start asking that question, you begin to see that:

- When your spouse only lets your child go outside with a mask or gloves a for a short amount of time each day during the pandemic, they're looking for a feeling of safety.
- When your spouse asks for an insane amount of maintenance or child support, they're often looking for security.
- When your spouse, who took no interest in the child before the divorce, now wants equal or even primary custody, they're often looking for respect and equality.

You know this person well and you're in an excellent position to see these deeper motivations, but you don't have the clarity to do this if you're browbeating, rage texting, or firing off threats. You have to be calm to get a useful emotional reading of the situation. The problem is that in a divorce, you're highly susceptible to being emotionally hijacked because your spouse is pushing your buttons. That's why I've put so much emphasis on emotional cooling tools like the 24-Hour Pause. In the heat of the moment, when you're only focusing on your own emotional reactions to the argument or negatively judging and criticizing your spouse, you can't tap into your emotional intelligence and let persuasion work its magic. Reacting emotionally essentially just leads to more battles.

However, when you have a conscious process for calming and detaching from the grip of your fear, anger, or outrage, you put yourself in a position to observe, listen, and recognize the needs behind your spouse's demands. In doing that, you become highly persuasive.

Here's a game plan to help you pull the plug on knee-jerk reactiveness and tap the skills of persuasion.

Step 1: Use the Hard Reset

When you are emotionally hijacked, the last place you want to be is in your head. When your mind is spinning, your rational powers are offline, and just like your phone, sometimes you need a hard reset to get back to normal functioning. The good news about the hard-reset technique is that it's quick and easy to do.

The bad news is that you will feel uncomfortable while doing it—but that's the point: you need to feel uncomfortable to snap out of your mind and into your body.

What do I mean by discomfort? Take a cold shower!

Seriously. It will change your state completely.

If you need to ease in, take a normal shower, and then during the last few minutes, gradually make the water colder and colder until it's uncomfortable. Try to stay for 15–30 seconds the first time and build up from there. You can end your shower with hot water before you dry off.

If you don't need a hard reset, you can also try its younger sibling, the soft reset, which involves focusing all your attention on wiggling your toes, the part of your body that's farthest away from your head.

You can also simply focus on your breathing. Slowly breathe in through your nose and out through your mouth, letting the breath flow in and out like the waves of the ocean. If you want some support for this, try something like The Breathing App (free for iOS and Android), which uses simple visuals and sounds to help tether you to your inhales and exhales.

Step 2: Remember, You Only Need to Be a Little Bit More Persuasive

Not even the best practitioners of persuasion are perfect, so give yourself permission to be imperfect at this tool.

To put this in perspective, and for illustration purposes only, realize that your spouse will most likely agree with about 40% of the issues you're requesting, and you'll most likely agree with about 40% of the issues that they are requesting. This is, of course, not a hard and fast number, but it is a useful way of thinking about the bigger picture. You only need to be about 11% more persuasive than you are now to gain an advantage, pushing that 40% to 51%.

Of course, this "last mile" of persuasion is not easy to do, but it is much easier than thinking you have to be an expert at persuasion in order to be effective.

Step 3: Visualize the Emotional Experience for an Edge

Starting out, you'll probably feel very unsure about trying to change your tactics with your spouse and upending the way you relate to conflict. You may think there is no use; this person will always want to battle.

To give yourself confidence as you learn the art of persuasion, first visualize the status quo and watch what happens to your emotions as you anticipate that your needs are not going to be met. Notice how your fear and anger rise. Replay how your spouse becomes provocative and baits you by acting out, raising their voice, as well as becoming disrespectful.

Visualize the negative emotional experience you have in this situation. This is what persuasion can change. Things don't have to stay this way.

Take a break to breathe. If you can't step away to do this, now's a good time to get out your breathing app or try a breathing exercise, something as simple as inhaling to a count of four and exhaling to a count of four. Doing this helps disengage your fight-or-flight response.

Now, visualize a positive experience. See yourself during this stressful time facing the familiar baiting from your spouse, but this time tuning it out and focusing on what you can control. Use the soft reset technique, concentrating on the rhythm of your breathing.

Then see yourself listening to a complaint or a triggering request from your spouse and using your emotional intelligence—your deep knowledge of who both of you are—to identify what each of you really needs in this situation.

What's the feeling each of you is looking for in the solution you're struggling to find? What deeper, positive need are you trying to satisfy?

As you breathe and visualize, you're creating space for your problem-solving brain to work so it can help you resolve the conflict. With curiosity and openness, you have the potential to enlist both your mind and your spouse's mind in order to find a creative solution.

Approaching the conflict this way, you'll be modeling an alternative to scorched-earth battles and inviting your spouse to join you in using it. It may strike them as puzzling or bizarre, but my experience tells me that it can also gently, even sneakily, persuade them to act from their best self and not their worst.

Case Study: How Vanessa Became Persuasive

Vanessa met Don when he was traveling abroad for work.

After several years of long-distance dating, they got married, and Vanessa moved to the U.S. to be with him. Soon after their marriage, they had a child, something they hadn't planned.

After Vanessa gave birth to their daughter, she felt something was off. Don wouldn't help her out with the baby. He wouldn't change a diaper or do a feeding in the middle of the night. He also expected Vanessa to cook for him and clean their home.

Vanessa started to feel more like a slave than a cherished spouse!

Vanessa and Don went to couples' therapy to try to resolve their differences, but Don dropped out after one session, and although Vanessa was hopeful things would change, they didn't.

Soon afterward, she asked for a divorce and said she wanted to move back home to Taiwan and take their child to be with her family there. Don resisted, and a custody battle ensued.

Only a few months into their divorce, the COVID pandemic hit, isolating Vanessa and Don together in their small NYC apartment.

Immediately, Vanessa told the child to wear a mask anytime she went out, but Don refused to wear a mask or make the child wear one when he went out with her. Since the laws at the time did not require mask wearing (which soon changed in many parts of the country), she realized that the only way to get Don to wear a mask and put one on the child was to become more persuasive.

However, Vanessa was so emotionally triggered by the events that she was not in the right state of mind to do that. She was thinking negatively—about Don's "failure as a parent," his "indifference to the child's safety," and so on—and these negative thoughts were being linked together like a chain around her neck that cut off all rational thinking.

She realized she needed a hard reset, so she followed the steps one by one, first taking a cold shower, then giving herself permission to be imperfect as she tried out new persuasion techniques.

Finally, she visualized her and Don's emotional reactions to these issues and thought about what was genuinely important to both parties. She saw that her emotional need was for caution, and his was for freedom and control.

Now, with her big brain—her reasoning power—back in charge, she came up with a game plan. She could create face masks on the kitchen table and make it an especially enjoyable experience for the child. Don would see what they were doing and also see how much fun their child was having putting together homemade masks.

She could also leave the materials out so Don could complete a mask himself. "She might not say anything up to that point, but if he saw how they worked, she could remark, "Look how much fun we're having making these masks!"

The next day, she could email Don and say, "We both want to protect the safety of our child and protect ourselves, and it seems that the countries that have the lowest incidence of outbreaks are wearing masks and the ones that are the most relaxed about not using masks have the highest outbreaks. What do you think we can do to ensure that we're doing everything possible to make sure our child is safe, given what's going on in the world?"

Even if she got a negative, nasty response to this question or Don ignored it, she'd stick firmly to the next step, which is to *do nothing*. Her primary goal was to offer Don a way to escape from his emotional hijacking and (hopefully) use his big brain too.

The "escape route" worked. The child was now interested in the masks and asking to wear them, which shifted the picture for everyone. No one was being "forced," and no negative words were being exchanged. Don could honor the child's freedom and still feel free himself; he got the *feeling* he wanted. He might even put on a mask his daughter had made for him. It was easier to do now, since it was his choice. It had become no big deal.

That's persuasion at work.

KEY POINTS: Becoming Persuasive

- Battling through problems is expensive. Even if you have the financial resources to hire an attorney to do your bidding, do you really have the budget (energy, emotion, and time) to spare on battling through every issue that comes up in divorce?
- Increasing your chances of prevailing in your divorce depends on learning to ease up on combat tactics and to be more persuasive.
- Start with the inner work, calming yourself and visualizing the experience you want. Identify the feeling that your spouse's request or position represents. Then, open yourself to the power of persuasion by finding ways to offer emotional support to them.

Conclusion
Putting It All Together

AS I WRAPPED UP this book on difficult divorces, my editor told me to keep the conclusion short. In following her sage advice, I thought I'd collect all of my key points in one place. They can help you maintain a strategic focus in your divorce and provide you with skills and methods that will help you get through it without losing your mind.

You can think of these key points as a foundation to build your way out of your high-conflict divorce. These are the same tools I share with my clients, and they've also led to my evolution both personally and professionally. I hope they will bring you greater calm, confidence, and ease in your divorce—and in the new life you'll create when it's over.

How the Divorce Team Works

- Your lawyer plays the outer game of the divorce. You play the inner game. FYI, the inner game of the divorce is 80% of the battle.
- You need a lawyer who is more interested in giving you good advice than in selling time. Racking up attorney fees does not necessarily lead to a better divorce, but good advice—which is not time dependent—may be priceless.

Why You Need to Ace the Emotional Game in Your Divorce

- A typical divorce focuses on solutions. A difficult divorce focuses on the unresolved emotional conflict.
- Leading first with solution-focused strategies when there is unresolved emotional conflict will often lead to escalation or deadlock.
- The goal is not to fight with the emotional side of your spouse, but to find better choreography to move past stalemates, roadblocks, and dead ends.

How You'll Get through This

- The first step in a divorce is prioritizing what is important to you and focusing on your priorities even if that means you may not get everything you want in your divorce.
- You may need to take a big step out of the situation you're in to plan for a better postdivorce life, and this process may be accelerated by professionals. Wounds heal better with proper care.
- Use the tools in the Emotional Survival Kit to cool any tendencies to react first and think later.
- Staying single-minded about your most important goals will empower you to push through when you hit that inevitable divorce wall.

Conclusion

- The focus should always be on what you can control. Unfortunately, you can't control your spouse, but you *can influence his or her behavior.*

How to Pace Yourself Mentally and Emotionally

- Understand that even if you "win" the divorce battle in front of you, you're in a long, drawn-out campaign with high costs to both sides. If you fight the emotional battles rather than the strategic ones, what you may wind up with is a pyrrhic victory as the cost outweighs the benefits.

- Three principles to always remember: Never act on your impulses when triggered. Never act on your impulses when triggered. Never act on your impulses when triggered.

- The game of a difficult divorce is like the game of chess. Even when you think all is lost, it is not over until the game has ended.

- When the heat is on, your only goal should be—in most cases—not to escalate matters. This is done primarily by focusing on self-care.

What to Know about Persuasion

- Defensiveness is a dead-on-arrival strategy in a difficult divorce because it is not persuasive or offensive.

- Persuasiveness starts when you take your spouse's perspective rather your own, so work first on seeing things their way, with the most positive perspective possible. You and your spouse *do have common ground.*
- Ask open-ended clarifying questions that make your spouse have to think with the analytical side of their brain. You know you're doing this right when there is a pause—even a slight one—before they answer.
- Give yourself permission to learn the tools and techniques of persuasion at your own pace and realize that these tools, even if perfectly used, are not 100% effective.

What to Know about Your Budget

- The divorce budget is made up of four categories, emotion, energy, time, and money. The higher the emotion involved, the higher the budget.
- The positive aspect of the energy budget is that it is renewable.
- Time is the most precious resource because it is not renewable.

How to Understand Divorce Lawyers

- The Swarmer focuses on draining your energy budget.

Conclusion

- The Brawler focuses on efficient case-ending facts like a "gotcha" Perry Mason moment.
- The Boxer focuses on efficiency.
- The Top Dog can do all styles well, but unless the divorce is one of the bigger ones in the office, most of the time you will be pawned off to a back-up associate, who may have the ego of the Top Dog, but not the bark or bite.

The One Thing You Need to Know about the Court

- Rule 1: the court is always right. When the court is wrong, see Rule 1.
- Courts generally prefer settlement.
- A court's decisions depend a lot on how the court views a party.

How to Recognize a Trusted Advisor

- Divorce attorneys have no financial incentive to contain costs, so you need to steer toward the ones who view themselves as trusted advisors rather than experts for hire.
- You know you hired an expert for hire when most of the advice focuses on selling time, meaning most of the advice focuses on time-consuming tactics that will run up the clock and cost you more.
- It's always helpful to get a second opinion to make sure that the suggestions you've already received are the best course.

Acknowledgments

To Bridget Farrington: this ride would not have been possible (or worthwhile) without you.

To my family and friends: thank you for your love and understanding and for all the joy you have given me.

To my clients past and present: my pride in you and appreciation of you is boundless.

I am so grateful to the super team I put together to bring my first book to life—especially Cindy Barrilleaux and Donna Frazier Glynn, who changed my mindset about writing. Many thanks also to Brijit Reed and Susan Shankin, who pushed me through the door to get this book out into the world.

About the Author

COREY SHAPIRO is a divorce attorney, mediator, and divorce strategist in New York City. He has guided thousands of people through difficult divorces, teaching them the secrets of getting through the process without losing their minds, and helping them emerge with the best chances for long-term happiness. Corey was a child of divorce. His life was upended when he came home from school as a third grader to learn that his mother had abandoned her family. That experience and what followed inspired him to enter family law and write Getting Divorced Without Losing Your Mind.

In addition to his work in private practice, Corey is a court-appointed mediator for the most difficult high conflict divorce cases. He shares his insight in a podcast, newsletter and crash course divorce workshop.

To send Corey feedback please email him at feedback@gettingdivorced.org.

www.ingramcontent.com/pod-product-compliance
Lightning Source LLC
LaVergne TN
LVHW041338080426
835512LV00006B/510